P9-DNB-842

JOB SEEKER SECRETS
MAKING THE INTERNET WORK FOR YOU

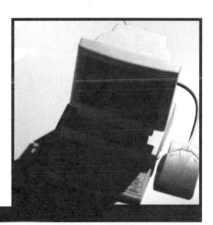

THOMAS J. FERRARA
INTERNET RECRUITING AND HUMAN CAPITAL ADVISOR AND CONSULTANT
FOUNDER AND FORMER PRESIDENT AND CEO OF CAREERENGINE, INC.

www.jobseekersecrets.com

THOMSON
SOUTH-WESTERN

OUACHITA TECHNICAL COLLEGE

Australia · Canada · Mexico · Singapore · Spain · United Kingdom · United States

THOMSON

SOUTH-WESTERN

Job Seeker Secrets: Making the Internet Work for You
by Thomas J. Ferrara

Editor-in-Chief:
Jack Calhoun

Vice President/Executive Publisher:
Dave Shaut

Team Leader:
Karen Schmohe

Aquisitions Editor:
Joseph Vocca

Project Manager:
Laurie Wendell

Director of Marketing:
Carol Volz

Marketing Manager:
Chris McNamee

Marketing Coordinator:
Lori Pegg

Production Editor:
Colleen A. Farmer

Writing and Editorial Services:
Vandalay Group Inc.
Cincinnati, Ohio

Production Manager:
Patricia Matthews Boies

Manufacturing Coordinator:
Kevin L. Kluck

Cover and Internal Designer:
Tippy McIntosh

Editorial Assistant:
Stephanie L. White

Production Assistant:
Nancy Stamper

Compositor:
Navta Associates, Inc.

Printer:
Edward Brothers, Ann Arbor

Instructor's Resource CD Developer:
Vandalay Group Inc.
Cincinnati, Ohio

Illustration Credit:
Artville Technology Icons
CD by Jeff Nishinaka,
© Artville, LLC

For permission to use material from this text, contact us by

Tel: (800) 730-2214
Fax: (800) 730-2215
Web: www.thomsonrights.com

For more information, contact South-Western, 5191 Natorp Boulevard, Mason, OH, 45040. Or you can visit our Internet site at www.swep.com.

Please note that the Internet addresses mentioned in this book were current and active at the time of publication. The Web sites are not affiliated with South-Western/Thomson Learning and are subject to change without notice.

STAND OUT IN THE CROWD!

Job Seeker Secrets: Making the Internet Work for You offers you the advice and tips to use when posting your resume online. Packed with information on today's top career sites, this one-of-a-kind text will give you the logic needed to gain the advantage. Enter the fast-paced world of job boards, career sites, and online resumes and take the first step to finding your new career.

Text   0-538-72666-0

Unlock the possibilities...with these additional career resources from South-Western. Do you need career enhancement, or additional practice with the latest technologies? We have the tools that will put you at the top of your field.

★ ### Online Training for the Administrative Professional
by Jennings, Stulz, and Rigby
This web-based program is the ideal distance education course or online supplement to today's office skills curriculum. Divided into 12 independent modules, this course will give administrative professionals the skills they need for success.

Visit www.swonlineoffice.com for 10-day FREE trial access!

★ ### Your Career: How to Make It Happen 5e
by Levitt
This market-leading text will teach you everything there is to know about finding a career. From networking to changing careers, this text details the steps necessary for success. Tips and advice, coupled with outstanding web-support from leading author Julie Levitt, give you the resources needed to succeed in any career.

Text/CD Package	0-538-72708-X
WebTutor for WebCT	0-538-72712-8
WebTutor for Blackboard	0-538-72713-6

★ ### The World of Customer Service
by Odgers
Designed for public or private, domestic or international organizations, this text will provide coverage on the basics of customer service, the use of technology, and how to professionally handle difficult customers. Problem solving guidelines and workplace profiles give useful information on a variety of topics such as attitude, education, and work experience.

Text/CD Package   0-538-72668-7

★ ### Call Centers: Technology & Techniques
by Green
Learn how to develop the necessary communication, interpersonal, and problem-solving skills needed for success. Designed for professionals working or interested in working as a call-center, customer service, or help-desk representative or manager, this text will focus on the soft-skill effectiveness of handling customers.

Text/CD Package   0-538-72686-5

THOMSON
SOUTH-WESTERN

Join us on the Internet at www.swep.com

Welcome to Job Seeker Secrets

Online job hunting and recruiting is a relatively new Internet revolution. Often cited as one of the best applications, or "killer apps," of the Internet, e-recruiting's growth and success near that of e-mail and e-commerce. By some estimates, over 50,000,000 people search for jobs through the Internet. Why? Because the Internet helps millions of people create, store, access, and exchange information in a way that no other medium can.

Let's think about that number: There are 50,000,000 people using the Internet to search for jobs, *at the same time you are*. But they can't all be searching for the job *you* want, right? True, but even factoring in geographic preferences, job types, and other such details, you're probably still competing against thousands of people.

How can you hold your own against such fierce competition? Be at the right place at the right time (or in our case, have your resume seen by the company recruiter precisely when he or she is looking for someone exactly like you). There are millions of resumes in online databases, and tens of thousands are added every day. With this book, *yours* will be the resume the recruiters see and *you* will be the candidate they hire.

Embarking on a job search is like learning to fish: There are many places to go and many techniques to use to increase your success. With this book as your guide, you'll be reeling in the jobs in no time!

- ❒ *Chapter 1:* Before you map the course of your Internet job search, you'll need to understand the scope of what you're about to undertake, the resources at your disposal, and techniques that will ensure success. Chapter 1 is an important introduction to these issues and a general discussion about Internet job seekers and Internet recruiters. A Guide to Essential Internet Terminology is included at the end of this chapter.

- ❒ *Chapter 2:* The first step to catching a fish is determining which type of fish you want to catch. In Chapter 2, you'll create a list of the types of jobs that best fit your interests and skills. This career target list will be the initial focus of your Internet job search.

- ❒ *Chapter 3:* Next, you'll need to work on your bait. In Chapter 3, you will learn how to fill your job-search "tackle box" with a variety of computer-friendly resumes and cover letters.

- ❒ *Chapter 4:* The best bait in the world is useless if you don't know how to fish. In Chapter 4, you'll learn basic and advanced Internet searching techniques for finding online job postings and for searching within a variety of job boards and career Web sites.

- ❒ *Chapter 5:* Some lakes stock more fish than others, and the more fish in the lake, the better your chances of catching one. In Chapter 5, you'll discover the advantages and disadvantages of using job boards, including evaluating them and registering profiles and resumes.

- **Chapter 6:** Often, the best way to catch a fish is to let someone with more experience do the work for you. In Chapter 6, you'll discover proven strategies for going directly to corporate sites and third-party recruiters.

- **Chapter 7:** The best anglers are experts about their local lakes. In Chapter 7, you'll learn to target your Internet job search to your desired locations.

- **Chapter 8:** Some lakes tend to house specific types of fish. In Chapter 8, you'll discover strategies for using job sites geared to specific careers and diverse job seekers.

- **Chapter 9:** It's the rare angler who catches the best fish on the first try. In Chapter 9, you'll discover how to keep the cupboard full and enhance your resume by finding online freelance jobs in your career field.

- **Chapter 10:** Sometimes you don't catch a fish on your first (or even second or third) try. When that happens, it's time to re-evaluate your bait and your techniques. You may even need the assistance of a fishing coach. In Chapter 10, you'll find tips for refining your Internet job search along with information about using professional career and resume services.

- **Web Site Directory:** Knowing which lakes to fish can make the difference between an empty stringer and a full one. The helpful directory at the end of this book will save you countless hours of research by providing you with quick access to the best destinations.

Features of this Text

Through the chapters and activities in this book, you'll discover how Internet job sites work, understand the logic behind them, and use this knowledge to create an advantage for yourself. You'll learn and practice proven techniques for every kind of Internet job seeker—senior executives and recent graduates, "techies" and Internet novices. Special sections and features in the chapters provide helpful resources to aid your quest for that new career opportunity.

- **Model Job Seekers** introduce the chapters and demonstrate ongoing examples of diverse job searches.

- **It's a Wrap** summarizes the key points of the chapter for quick reference.

- **Learn the Lingo** provides exercises in learning employment and Internet terminology.

- **E-valuation** presents additional projects and activities for self-assessment and extended practice with job search techniques.

- **5 Star Web Sites** highlight important Web sites to visit for career development and job search resources.

- ❏ *Ethics and Etiquette* addresses privacy concerns and the proper etiquette of online recruiting and job application.
- ❏ *Fact or Myth?* debunks Internet myths and "get rich quick" schemes.
- ❏ *Now You Know* and *Stats* provide up-to-date statistics and trends in technology and recruiting.

Tips from the Pros

In every chapter, you'll get firsthand advice from the "pros" of the industry—the industry leaders and engineers who have provided their knowledge of what works and what doesn't. Insights and information from the following contributors can be found in the features called "Tips from the Pros."

- **Jeff Taylor:** Founder and Chairman, Monster® (**www.monster.com**)
- **Henry Neils:** President and Founder, Assessment.com (**www.assessment.com**)
- **Jennifer Floren:** CEO and Founder, Experience.com, Inc. (**www.experience.com**)
- **Samer Hamadeh:** President and CEO, Vault Inc. (**www.vault.com**)
- **Peter Newfield:** President, Career Resumes (**www.career-resumes.com**)
- **Todd Miller:** Founder and CEO, SalesHeads℠ (**www.salesheads.com**)
- **Dwaine Maltais:** Vice President of e-Recruiting Solutions, Bernard Hodes Group (**www.hodes.com**)
- **David Bacharach:** President, CS Information Technologies (**www.careersearch.net**)
- **Scott Scanlon:** Chairman and CEO, Hunt-Scanlon Advisors (**www.hunt-scanlon.com**)
- **Chris Miller:** Founder and Former CEO, 6FigureJobs.com™ (**www.6figurejobs.com**)
- **Jason Krebs:** Vice President of Sales and General Manager, *The New York Times* on the Web (**www.nytimes.com**)
- **Mark F. Weinberg:** Chief Operating Officer, CareersInGovernment, Inc. (**www.careersingovernment.com**)
- **Bob Wallach:** CEO, MarketingPower.com, a subsidiary of the American Marketing Association (**www.marketingpower.com**)
- **Bradford Rand:** Founder and CEO, Job Expo International, Inc. (**www.job-expo.com**)
- **Dan Cahn:** Founder, WorkLife Solutions, Inc. (**www.worklife.com**)

JobSeekerSecrets.com

JobSeekerSecrets.com is a valuable online resource that has been created from the research and development of this text. This site provides its members with both a free service and an optional paid subscription service. (All areas are free to purchasers of this text.)

- ❏ *Free access to:* job search advice, tips and career development content, newsletters, top ranked resources, screened service providers, message boards, and more
- ❏ *Paid access to:* book content and exercises, job board reviews, and a comprehensive job board/job search directory

Instructor's Resource CD

An Instructor's Resource CD is available for instructors using *Job Seeker Secrets*. This helpful instructor tool contains the following resources.

- ❏ chapter descriptions and outlines
- ❏ teaching suggestions
- ❏ additional assignments and worksheets
- ❏ solutions to activities
- ❏ links to Web resources
- ❏ sample resumes and cover letters
- ❏ PowerPoint® slides for lecture and discussion

About the Author

Who is better suited to reveal the secrets of e-recruiting than one of the leaders and engineers of the industry? Tom Ferrara is a seasoned online recruiting and e-commerce veteran. He has been a consultant and advisor to numerous high-profile Internet destinations and software companies. Recently, Tom was the executive vice president of CareerHarmony, Inc., an international company that provides corporations with global screening and assessment solutions. Previously, Tom was the founder, president, and CEO of CareerEngine Inc., one of the first and leading companies to power career sites on the Internet. In addition to its technology offering, CareerEngine has one of the largest networks of category-specific career sites on the Internet, which is sold to and represented by over 60 of the largest recruitment advertising companies in the world. Tom is commonly called upon for his expertise in human capital and has

been featured as a speaker at various e-recruiting trade shows and workshops. In addition to offering expert commentary to numerous news-based Web sites, Tom has regularly appeared on TV segments and in over 50 newspapers, magazines, and trade publications, such as CNN, ABC, NBC, *The Wall Street Journal*, *Los Angeles Times*, *Chicago Tribune*, and *Investor's Business Daily*. Additionally, Tom has consulted with some of the world's largest newspapers, search firms, staffing firms, magazines, portals, and generalist career sites regarding their operations, industry awareness, user interfaces, effectiveness, and growth of market share.

Author's Acknowledgments

I would like to specifically thank "The Pros" who so generously contributed their wisdom and advice to this book: Jeff Taylor, Henry Neils, Jennifer Floren, Samer Hamadeh, Peter Newfield, Todd Miller, Dwaine Maltais, David Bacharach, Scott Scanlon, Chris Miller, Jason Krebs, Mark F. Weinberg, Bob Wallach, Bradford Rand, and Dan Cahn.

I'd also like to acknowledge the premiere Internet services that granted permission to reprint images from their Web sites: Monster, 6FigureJobs.com, Assessment.com, CareersInGovernment, Entrepreneur.com, Google, Percepta LLC, FlipDog.com, ClickCity.com, Vault.com, Hunt-Scanlon Corporation, MarketingPower, Inc., Yahoo! Inc., Artemis International Solutions Corporation, and the U.S. Bureau of Labor Statistics.

Thank you to Elizabeth Skipper, Lesa Petersen, Emily Roots, Anita Buck, and Lauri Harwood of Vandalay Group Inc. for their expert development and editorial services and to the publishing staff of South-Western/ Thomson.

Finally, I am most grateful for the love and support of my family: my wife Julie, son Dylan, daughter Emily, and cat Sasha, my father Nick, my mother Monika, Gil, Janet, Nick Jr., Katherine, Christine, Christopher, Jennifer, and Rick. Thanks also to my associates and friends who provided special assistance during this project: Matt Blumenthal, Mike Susi, Neil S., Ken K., Janine W., Shirly W., Pete G. & Bobo.

Reviewers

The author and publisher wish to recognize the following instructors who gave valuable feedback and constructive criticism during the development of the *Job Seeker Secrets* manuscript:

- Susan B. Pehl, Modesto Junior College, Modesto, CA
- Candace B. Schiffer, M.A., Tri-State Business Institute, Erie, PA
- Laurie Shapero, Miami-Dade Community College, Miami, FL
- Brian Sporleder, Bryant & Stratton College, Milwaukee, WI

TABLE OF CONTENTS

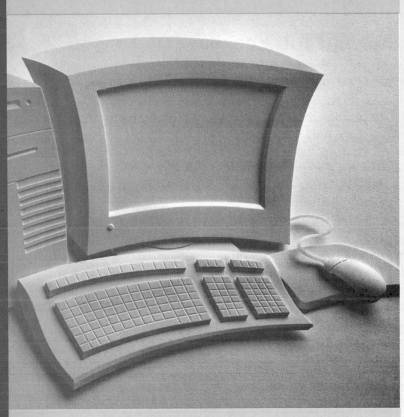

CHAPTER OBJECTIVES

❏ Discover how an Internet job search differs from a traditional job search.

❏ Understand why and how employers and recruiters use the Internet to recruit employees.

CHAPTER 1

THE INTERNET AND THE JOB SEEKER

Online recruiting is one of the fastest-growing applications of the Internet. Today, more than 90 percent of college graduates will look for work on the Internet, while fewer than 10 percent looked for work on the Internet only 10 years ago. Likewise, today's employers are hiring about 40 percent of their workforce through the Internet; and those numbers are growing quickly. Millions of employers and job seekers are taking advantage of the Internet's capacity to connect people in hopes of finding a match.

   As an Internet job seeker, you'll need a basic understanding of how an online job search differs from a traditional job search. This chapter will present an overview of what makes an Internet job seeker successful and why and how employers look for candidates through the Internet.

Learn the Lingo

New to the Internet? A helpful guide for Internet newcomers (and a reference for veterans) is provided at the end of this chapter. Here, you'll learn terminology that is crucial for your Internet job search.

The Internet Job Seeker

Internet job seekers come in all shapes and sizes. A job seeker who works in a high-demand field, such as network administration or computer programming, might rely on Internet recruiting to find the most competitive salaries. A job seeker who is relocating to a new city might want to save time and effort by looking for Internet job postings in the new location before the move. A job seeker who works in a **niche field** (a rare and/or highly specialized career field), such as manual book binding or movie sound editing, may need to turn to the Internet to find work specific to his or her skills.

Fortunately, online job-searching methods are as abundant and diverse as Internet job seekers. Whether you're a senior executive or a recent graduate, a "techie" or an Internet novice, the Internet can provide you with a variety of exciting career opportunities.

Job Searches: Traditional vs. Internet

For the purposes of this book, a **traditional job search** refers to a job search that doesn't use the Internet, and an **Internet job search** refers to a job search that *principally* uses the Internet to find and respond to job listings. In essence, a traditional job search describes what job searches were like prior to the Internet.

Though a small percentage of the workforce performs job searches without the use of any Internet function—including e-mail—those numbers are decreasing by the day. Most job searches combine aspects of both the traditional job search and the Internet job search. By performing your job search primarily via the Internet, you will be among the fast-growing pioneers of cyber job-hunting.

NOW YOU KNOW

The Internet and the World Wide Web are not the same entity. The Internet is simply a channel for digital information, such as digital pictures, sounds, numbers and words. The World Wide Web is not the entire Internet, but one (very large) application of the Internet. The World Wide Web shares data, such as Web pages, in the form of HTML, or hypertext markup language.

E-mail, listservs (online discussion groups), and instant messaging are all examples of Internet applications that don't rely on the use of HTML. (See "Know What You're Talking About: Essential Internet Terminology" at the end of this chapter.)

Figure 1.1 contrasts the basic elements of traditional and Internet job searches. The interview process is the only part of an Internet job search that mirrors a traditional job search (though a small percentage of employers are beginning to conduct online interviews).

Job Seekers...	Traditional Job Search	Internet Job Search
Find job listings from:	• Newspaper classified ads • Trade or industry journals • Career placement centers • "Now Hiring" signs	• Online job boards • Corporate Web sites • Online newspapers • Regional employment Web sites • Industry, niche, diversity, non-profit, and government Web sites • Online newsgroups and bulletin boards
Respond to job listings by:	• Mailing or personally delivering a paper resume and cover letter • Filling out a paper application form	• E-mailing an electronic resume and cover letter • Completing an online application form
Create resumes that are:	• Formatted with boldface, italics, centering, and bullets • Printed on resume paper	• Plain-text (not formatted) • Packed with career-related keywords • Sent electronically
Create cover letters that are:	• Typically three paragraphs long • Formatted with basic graphic elements • Printed on resume paper	• One (short) paragraph in length • Sent as e-mail text
Contact employers:	• By telephone • By mail • In person	• By e-mail

Figure 1.1 Traditional Job Searches vs. Internet Job Searches

Tips from the Pros

by Jeff Taylor
Founder and Chairman, Monster® (www.monster.com)

The concept of online job searching has changed greatly since the beginning, when job Web sites were simply bulletin boards. Today, the Internet is the gateway to a better job and a better life, as you can manage your entire career online. At Monster®, we view ourselves as a comprehensive career management resource, serving job seekers from interns to CEOs. We offer much more than just a listing of jobs. By utilizing all the available resources, including expert advice on interviewing and building your resume, you can maximize the potential of your online job search and make yourself more marketable in the process.

To begin your online job search, you first need to post your resume. Once you do so, employers can come and find you. The next step is to target your region and area of interest. You can search in specific regions within each state and according to job category. Once you find a job of interest, you can apply directly online with your newly-created resume. And Monster® can also do additional work for you: Create a job search agent with the region and job category specified, and Monster® will e-mail you opportunities that match your criteria.

There are millions of people on the Internet, so to be successful, you must be persistent and smart—follow up on an application, make sure to send thank-you letters, and confidently project yourself as an invaluable candidate who would be an asset to any company; the speed of the Internet is not a substitute for the manners that we have learned over the years about searching for jobs. Online resources can not only give you available opportunities, but they can also make you a more desirable candidate and help you obtain your dream job!

Jeff Taylor is the founder and chairman of Monster® and the global director of Interactive, TMP Worldwide Inc., the parent company of Monster®. He has an executive MBA/OPM from the Harvard Business School and an undergraduate degree from the University of Massachusetts at Amherst. Through Jeff's guidance and leadership, Monster® catapulted to the number one position in the online careers industry, currently serving over 17 million job seekers each month. Today, the Monster® global network consists of local content and language sites in 21 countries.

© 2002. Used with permission of the author.

Figure 1.2 Monster® Home Page
©2002 Monster. Reprinted by permission.

What the Internet Will Do for the Job Seeker

The best reason to conduct your job search over the Internet is *abundance*. No other place, system, or practice in the history of job searching has provided job seekers with such a wealth of career opportunities.

- ☐ ***The Internet will offer scores of job listings.*** Compared to traditional job search listings, the number of Internet listings is staggering.

- ☐ ***The Internet will provide many different job search avenues.*** Job seekers can fine-tune their searches according to job titles, industries, geography, and companies.

- ☐ ***The Internet will be a warehouse of free career advice and information.*** Many career-related Web sites offer help, answer common questions, and provide useful links for job seekers.

What the Internet Won't Do for the Job Seeker

Though the Internet offers countless job listings and search avenues, it's a common fallacy that a job seeker can simply post his or her resume online and be instantly besieged with thousands of great job offers. Even job seekers in high-demand careers must do a bit of work before the phone begins to ring off the hook.

- ☐ ***The Internet won't conduct your job search for you.*** Though resumes received countless hits during the beginning stages of online recruiting, there are millions of resumes online today. You'll need to do some work to make yourself stand out in the crowd.

- ☐ ***The Internet won't accept traditional job-hunting practices.*** If you want to win the game, you'll need to play by the rules. Your resumes, cover letters, and employer correspondence should be in line with Internet job searching standards and etiquette.

- ☐ ***The Internet won't place your ideal career in your lap.*** Though there are innumerable job listings on the Internet, a simple click of the mouse won't make your ideal job appear in flashing lights. You'll need to know exactly what you're looking for and how to find it, and you'll need to put some work into finding it.

How Long Will My Internet Job Search Take?

If you know what you're doing—and you *will* after you read and complete the chapters in this book—your Internet job search should take much less time than a traditional job search. The average traditional job search in a stable economy will take one to six months, depending on your career. In an unstable economy, a traditional job search may take two months to a year.

If you are in a high-demand career field, such as network administration, your Internet job search may only take a couple of days! (That is, of course, after you have created your computer-friendly resumes and learned effective search methods.) The average Internet job search will take between two days and six weeks, depending on the following factors.

❏ Your career field
❏ Your level of employment (executive, entry-level, etc.)

❏ Your location
❏ The economy

Figure 1.3 shows the average maximum length, in days, of traditional and Internet job searches.

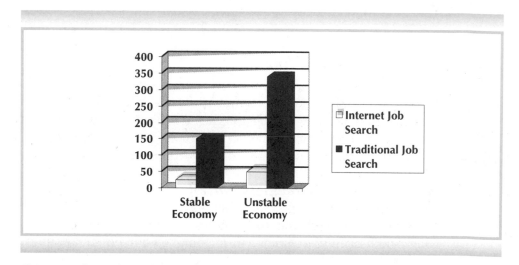

Figure 1.3 Job Search Length in Days

What Makes a Successful Internet Job Seeker?

Successful Internet job seekers have all of the attributes and tools of successful traditional job seekers. The difference lies in applying those attributes to the specific requirements of an Internet job search.

❏ Knowledge of their career fields
❏ An understanding of what they want and what they're worth
❏ Effective resumes and cover letters
❏ An understanding of job searching etiquette and practices
❏ A professional attitude
❏ Organizational skills
❏ Determination and patience

Necessary Tools

In addition to the necessary attributes, Internet job seekers must be equipped with the following tools.

- ❏ **Easy access to the Internet:** It may seem obvious, but the essential idea here is *easy* Internet access. If you are not online at home, find a computer with an Internet connection that you can use for two to four hours at a time, three to five times per week. (Check with your school; a friend; a cyber café; a copy center; or your local library if its time limits are not restrictive.)

- ❏ **A personal e-mail account:** E-mail will be your primary means of communication during your Internet job search. It will also be your primary method of sending resumes and cover letters. Therefore, you will *absolutely* need a personal e-mail account, preferably one with a professional, straightforward address (e.g., *martinb@vision.net*; *paula21@bluemarble.com*). Many employers are put off by e-mail addresses with amusing nicknames or popular culture references (e.g., *h_dawg@viking.net*; *malibu_grrrrl@yahoo.com*). Once you start applying for jobs online, you should check your e-mail at least once every day.

- ❏ **Easy access to a computer that has word processing software:** To get your resume in shape for your Internet job search, you'll need easy access to a computer that has commonly used word-processing software, such as Microsoft Word. You'll also need the software to compose e-mail cover letters before you paste them into e-mail text. (You'll want to print and check them for errors before you send them.)

> "Thanks to the Internet, answering want ads has become a job search method on steroids. On many sites, including **Monster.com**, you can even have an electronic job scout scour the Net for you 24/7, ...delivering the best fits on a silver platter right to your electronic door."
>
> –Marty Nemko
> Columnist, Career Advisor Host of "Work with Marty Nemko" on National Public Radio

Career Fields

One of the main concerns about Internet job searching is that the jobs are all geared toward high-tech fields. Many job seekers feel that online job listings are for "techies" only. It's true that roughly 50 percent of online job board listings are technical, computer-related jobs. However, the other 50 percent—which includes job listings in communications, health-care, marketing, and more—is growing rapidly. It's also important to understand that the job boards are only one of many ways to find online job advertisements.

The most commonly advertised career fields on the job board sites are:

- ❏ Technical, including computer programming and systems administration
- ❏ Engineering
- ❏ Financial services
- ❏ Accounting
- ❏ Sales and marketing

- ❑ Administrative
- ❑ Telecommunications
- ❑ Retail
- ❑ Communications and public relations
- ❑ Teaching and academic research
- ❑ Business and professional services
- ❑ Executive
- ❑ Healthcare
- ❑ Legal

Plenty of non-technical positions are found through corporate Web sites and other job search methods, which you'll learn about throughout this book. That means that *anyone*—a technical guru or a professional basket weaver—can find work on the Internet, including *you*!

Are You a Passive or an Active Job Seeker?

In order to plan your Internet job search strategy, you need to determine whether you are a passive job seeker or an active job seeker. This distinction will influence how concerned you should be about the **confidentiality** of your information (its availability to specific employers) when applying for Internet jobs.

Passive Job Seekers

A **passive job seeker** is generally defined as someone who is employed but is *passively* looking for a better opportunity. A passive job seeker has a position and therefore doesn't *need* a new job. Passive job seekers are open to better opportunities and will willingly change jobs when an ideal position comes along. They must, however, be particularly careful about

Please Choose One: *

⦿ **Option 1:**   I would like my information to be entered into your searchable database.

Make My Information Available to: ☑ Executive Recruiters ☑ Employers

○ **Option 2:**   My confidentiality is of the utmost importance and I do not want my information posted or disseminated in any way.

Auto Email Job Alerts that match your resume posting. How does this work?   Yes ○ No ○

If you have chosen Option 1 you may choose what contact information is made available to Employers and Executive Recruiters. Check Yes or No from the column along the right side with regard to whether you would like this line of information made available. At a minimum we suggest you make available your First Name, State, and Email.

Figure 1.4 Online Resume Confidentiality Settings
© 2002 6FigureJobs.com. Reprinted by permission.

applying for jobs to avoid jeopardizing their current positions. The Internet makes it easy for employers to find out when employees are looking for new jobs, and employers are likely to dismiss employees who would rather work somewhere else. That's why passive job seekers often post their online resumes confidentially by not disclosing their contact information or company name.

ETHICS & ETIQUETTE

Employers routinely track employee e-mail usage. If you're a passive job seeker, *never* use your company e-mail address as a point of contact. Using your company resources for any personal reason can be cause for reprimand. Using your company e-mail to find a new job could initiate your dismissal.

Active Job Seekers

An **active job seeker** is generally defined as someone who is not employed and is *actively* looking for a job. Looking for work is the active job seeker's full-time occupation. Graduation is looming, and/or employment in a chosen career is needed in a short period of time. Active job seekers don't need to worry about confidentiality. There is no need to hide the fact that they're looking for work, because they're not in danger of jeopardizing their current (lack of) employment.

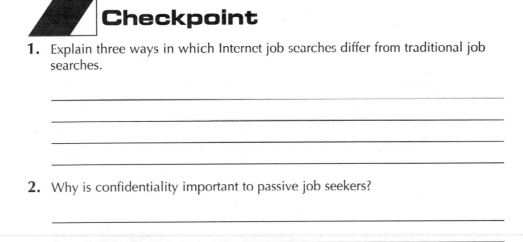

Checkpoint

1. Explain three ways in which Internet job searches differ from traditional job searches.

   _____

   _____

   _____

   _____

2. Why is confidentiality important to passive job seekers?

   _____

   _____

The Internet Recruiter

More and more employers are using the Internet to recruit employees for the same reason job seekers use the Internet: *abundance*. The Internet provides employers with many more potential employees than traditional job candidate searching methods, such as print newspaper advertisements.

But that's not the only reason that e-recruiting—the practice of finding candidates for job openings through the Internet—is a rapidly growing trend among today's employers.

❑ Employers can reach a wider spectrum of candidates.

❑ E-recruiting is typically less expensive than traditional methods.

❑ E-recruiting typically takes less time than traditional methods.

How the Internet Recruitment Process Works

When a company has a position to fill, it typically offers the position to internal candidates first (people who are already employed at the organization). If an appropriate candidate is not found within the company, the following events occur.

1. The human resources department or a person with the authority to hire searches a collected stack of resumes. The electronic version of a stack of resumes is a **resume database**, a computerized storage application for resumes that allows them to be searched by experience, education, job titles, and other elements. These resumes typically come from referrals to the company by connections with current employees. This is called **networking**, connecting with people or groups who can assist you in finding a job. Unsuccessful applications for previous positions and "cold" applications (resumes sent for general consideration, not in response to a particular listing) are also considered.

2. If an appropriate candidate is not found through internal resumes, an employer will do any combination of the following things.

   ❑ Place an advertisement on job board site(s) or online classifieds.

   ❑ Place an advertisement on the company's Web site.

   ❑ Hire a **third-party recruiter**, an outside party who works with companies to find candidates for positions that are difficult to fill.

Internal Recruiters

Internal recruiters work for the company that has the open position. Internal recruiters are typically human resources professionals, full-time employees who handle e-recruiting in addition to job responsibilities that are not related to hiring candidates. Human resources professionals are responsible for soliciting and narrowing down the preliminary stack of job candidates. They then forward a small number of suitable resumes to the person who has the authority to hire. A human resources professional will almost always manage the initial e-recruitment process for internal company job openings. However, there are some exceptions.

- ❒ In some small companies, the person who has the authority to hire manages all phases of the e-recruitment process.

- ❒ If a company is hiring an upper-level executive, the president or CEO may handle the e-recruitment process.

Third-Party Recruiters

Many companies will only use third-party recruiters when they feel they've exhausted their other options. Third-party recruiters provide a valuable service to companies in search of high-demand or high-tech candidates, upper-level executives and CEOs, or people in niche fields. They also come in handy when human resources professionals simply don't have the time to handle an extensive candidate search.

However, there is a price to pay for this valuable service. If a company hires a candidate provided by a third-party recruiter, that third-party recruiter will receive the equivalent of nearly 30 percent of the hired employee's first-year salary. (The salary isn't reduced; employers must pay that amount to third-party recruiters in addition to paying the new hire's full salary.) So, if you find an Internet job listing through a third-party recruiter, understand that you will be slightly less attractive to a potential employer than a candidate who applies directly to the company. If you are in high demand, however, there is little need to worry. Companies are willing to pay for the service of finding a first-rate employee like you. Chapters 5 and 6 will cover third-party recruiters in more detail.

 **Checkpoint**

1. Describe the two basic types of Internet recruiters.

_____

_____

2. List two reasons that an employer might hire a third-party recruiter.

_____

_____

ETHICS & ETIQUETTE

Job advertisements from internal recruiters and third-party recruiters are often used at the same time for the same position. Never try to side-step a third-party recruiter who has already contacted you about a position. Employers consider such behavior dishonest.

It's a Wrap

❏ Today, more than 90 percent of college graduates will look for work on the Internet, while fewer than 10 percent looked for work on the Internet only 10 years ago. Likewise, today's employers are hiring about 40 percent of their workforce through the Internet; and those numbers are growing quickly.

❏ Whether you're a senior executive or a recent graduate, a "techie" or an Internet novice, the Internet can provide you with a variety of exciting career opportunities.

❏ The Internet provides employers with many more potential employees than traditional job candidate searching methods. At the same time, e-recruiting is faster and cheaper than traditional searching methods.

> The fact remains that the overwhelming majority of people who have become wealthy have become so thanks to work they found profoundly absorbing. The long term study of people who eventually became wealthy clearly reveals that their 'luck' arose from accidental dedication they had to an arena they enjoyed.
>
> –Srully Blotnick
> Psychologist and *Forbes* columnist

Learn the Lingo

Match each term to its definition.

Terms

____ **1.** active job seeker   ____ **6.** niche field
____ **2.** confidentiality   ____ **7.** passive job seeker
____ **3.** e-recruiting   ____ **8.** resume database
____ **4.** Internet job search   ____ **9.** third-party recruiter
____ **5.** networking   ____ **10.** traditional job search

Definitions

a. a job search that uses no Internet function whatsoever

b. someone who is not employed in his or her chosen career and needs or wants work in a short period of time

c. electronic recruiting; the practice of finding candidates for job openings through the Internet

d. a computerized storage application for resumes that allows them to be searched by experience, education, job titles, and other elements

e. an outside party who works with companies to find candidates for positions that are difficult to fill

f. a career field that is both rare and highly specialized

g. someone who is currently employed and does not want or need employment right away, but is looking for a better opportunity

h. connecting with people or groups who can assist you in finding a job

i. a job search that primarily uses the Internet to find and respond to job listings

j. control over a specific employer's access to your information

> Your chances of success are directly proportional to the degree of pleasure you desire from what you do. If you are in a job you hate, face the fact squarely and get out.

–Michael Korda
Author, *Success!*

E-valuation

1. Think of some additional attributes that might be necessary for a successful Internet job search. Combine your list with the attributes cited in this chapter (patience, organizational skills, etc.). Distribute the list to friends who are looking for jobs on the Internet. Ask them to score themselves on each attribute on a scale of 1 to 5 (5 being highest). Tally the results, and answer the questions below.

    a. Which attributes are commonly lacking among Internet job seekers? Which attributes are strong?

    b. How did you score?

    c. What do you need to work on?

2. Conduct an Internet search to determine if your career field is well-represented on the job boards. Go to **www.monster.com** and/or **www.careerbuilder.com** and tally the number of jobs listed in your career field. (Listings don't need to be jobs that you're qualified to do.) Figure out the percentage of job listings in your career field based on the total number of jobs listed on the job board. (Most job boards regularly update these numbers.)

KNOW WHAT YOU'RE TALKING ABOUT:
ESSENTIAL INTERNET TERMINOLOGY

browser
A browser is a program, such as Microsoft Internet Explorer or Netscape Navigator, that enables users to receive and display Web pages.

bulletin board system
A bulletin board system is an electronic version of a community bulletin board (like the ones you find at supermarkets, school organizations, or community associations). There are innumerable bulletin boards for specialized groups on the Internet that allow users to post discussions, information, and often job openings.

directory
A directory is a database of Web pages that is created by human reviewers. Examples include Yahoo!® (**www.yahoo.com**) and LookSmart℠ (**www.looksmart.com**).

FAQ (Frequently Asked Questions)
Most Web sites post a list of frequently asked questions, commonly abbreviated as FAQ. FAQ pages can be great tools for finding information, troubleshooting problems, and learning the rules and etiquette for a particular Web site.

home page

1. A home page is the first page that opens when you log on to the Internet. This can be the Web page of your Internet Service Provider, or a Web page or Web site that you personally designate as the default opening page. When you click the *Home* button on your browser's status bar, it will take you here.

2. A home page can also be a Web site's opening page or main page. If you get lost within a Web site and want to return to the beginning of the site, click on the hyperlink that says *Home* or *Main*.

HTML
HTML is an abbreviation for hypertext markup language, the language used for creating Web sites.

hyperlink

A hyperlink is a word, phrase, or Web site address that is set off with separate colors and underlining, like this: hyperlink. Clicking on a hyperlink sends you to another Web page.

Internet Service Provider (ISP)

An Internet Service Provider is like a telephone company for the Internet. ISPs provide access to the Internet for a monthly fee. ISPs are also referred to as access providers, service providers, and connectivity providers.

job bank

A job bank stores job listings in a computer database that can be searched by keywords. Many types of job sites provide searchable job banks.

listserv

A listserv is a mailing list that receives participants' messages and resends them to subscribers via e-mail. Discussions and announcements, often sent in newsletter form, can be a great resource for job openings.

metalist

Also called meta indexes, metalists are Web sites or Web pages that provide massive "lists of lists," or links, to a variety of related subjects.

newsgroup

A newsgroup, like a listserv, receives participants' messages and distributes them to subscribers. Unlike listservs, newsgroups have strictly defined subject categories.

resume bank

A resume bank stores job seekers' resume listings in a computer database that can be searched by keywords. Many types of job sites provide searchable resume banks.

search engine

A search engine is a database of Web pages that is created by computer programs. Examples include AltaVista® (**www.altavista.com**) and Google™ (**www.google.com**).

URL (Uniform Resource Locator)

URL is the technical term for a Web site or Web page address. One Web site will have multiple URLs, which all stem from a base URL. (For example, **www.microsoft.com** is the URL for the home page of Microsoft's Web site. Specific pages within that Web site will have different URLs, such as **www.microsoft.com/downloads**.)

❐ Understand the importance of a career self-assessment.

❐ Expand your career possibilities by exploring your interests, skills, and possible industries.

❐ Prioritize your career possibilities by identifying the characteristics of your ideal career.

❐ Use your prioritized career possibilities to take a first look at job listings on the Internet.

KNOW WHAT YOU'RE LOOKING FOR

CHAPTER 2

Too often in job searches—and in life—we take "the easy road" by accepting what is right in front of us. Unfortunately, that strategy rarely leads to satisfaction in life or in work. What is the best way to get what you want? *Know* what you want. One of the most common—and dangerous—mistakes job seekers make is beginning a job search without a clear idea of what they're looking for. Before you can market yourself to an employer, you must know yourself well.

The Internet is a gateway to all kinds of work and millions of job postings. That's why knowing what you're looking for is *especially* important before you begin looking for jobs on the Internet. This chapter will help you develop a clear picture of your desired responsibilities, work environment, salary, and location in order to bring purpose and focus to your Internet job search. Narrowing down your search in this way will make the process easier, faster, and more productive.

Model Job Seeker

Our model job seeker for this chapter is Jamal. He's finishing his certification in veterinary technology and has experience walking dogs and working as an assistant in a veterinary clinic. Jamal is pursuing a career as a veterinary technician and enjoys classifying his rock collection and reading true-crime books in his spare time. Jamal's experiences with identifying his career possibilities are provided as examples throughout this chapter.

The Career Self-Assessment

When people meet you, they typically ask, "What do you do?" And often, when we describe friends or family members, we mention their professions—for instance, "He's a teacher," or "She owns a design firm." Why is this so? Because what you do for a living largely defines who you are: your talents, your personality, and what role your job plays in your life.

Unfortunately, very few people truly know what they want to do. Finding a satisfying career involves a serious evaluation of your work experience, talents, and career values—or what career experts commonly call a career **self-assessment**. A self-assessment is an evaluation tool that is designed to help you know yourself before you set your career goals and start down a path for meeting those goals.

Why Do You Need a Self-Assessment?

A popular saying claims, "Do what you love, and you'll love what you do." But how can you *do* what you love if you don't *know* what you love? That's where self-assessments come in. These tools can help you figure out what drives you and what you're passionate about—what you love.

If you've been in the workforce for a while, you might have a better idea of what you do and don't want than first-time job seekers or people beginning new careers. But even people with a lot of work experience can benefit from exploring the variety of ways they could apply their talents.

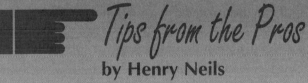

Tips from the Pros
by Henry Neils
President and Founder, Assessment.com
(www.assessment.com)

In today's job market, self-knowledge is the most important piece of a successful job search. To help you gain knowledge about different aspects of yourself, who you are, and what you want out of your life and your career, there are several types of motivational interest, workplace, and personality inventories that can be taken.

Explore your motivations as they apply to the world of work. A career assessment can point you in the right direction by showing which careers are right for you. Then narrow the search by studying the work environment to see if the work day would be satisfying to you. The most important result of your work is achieving personal satisfaction. The money will follow.

As Confucius said, "Get a job you love, and you will never have to work a day in your life."

Henry Neils is president and founder of Assessment.com, the leading online career assessment company focused on helping employees and employers work together for their mutual benefit. Millions of people have gained personal insight into their potential careers by using the tools, such as MAPP™ (Motivational Appraisal of Personal Potential), provided at Assessment.com.

© 2002. Used with permission of the author.

The Internet is not the only resource for self-assessments. The career counselor's office at your school or institution will typically provide you with free self-assessments.

Online Self-Assessments

An online career self-assessment can be a valuable enhancement to your comprehensive career self-assessment. There are numerous self-assessment Web sites that provide different insights on how personal interests and working personalities affect career satisfaction and success.

Online self-assessments also provide automatic score calculations. However, not all online self-assessments are useful, manageable, or reliable, and some may give you misleading results. The following sites contain self-assessments that are recommended by many online career resources and recruiters.

- ❏ The Career Key: **www.careerkey.org/english**
- ❏ The Keirsey Temperament Sorter II™: **www.advisorteam.com/user/ktsintro1.asp**
- ❏ Work Interest Quiz: **www.myfuture.com/career/interest.html**
- ❏ The Princeton Review® Career Quiz: **www.review.com/career/careerquizhome.cfm**
- ❏ MAPP™ (Motivational Appraisal of Personal Potential): **www.assessment.com**

MAPP™   Preference #2 of 71

Most ○ Least ○ Assemble and run a model railroad
Most ○ Least ○ Assemble a large complicated jig-saw puzzle
Most ○ Least ○ Work on a cross-word puzzle from a newspaper

Figure 2.1 Online Self-Assessment Question
© 2002 Assessment.com. Reprinted by permission.

 **Checkpoint**

List two advantages and one disadvantage of online self-assessments.

_____

_____

_____

Expanding Your Career Possibilities

As you expand your career possibilities, imagine yourself as a newcomer in a big city. You know your neighborhood pretty well, but you want to see what else the city has to offer. To get a thorough idea of the city's possibilities, you'll want to examine every restaurant, shop, museum, market, alley, and park bench that interests you. After your exploration, you'll have a variety of new opportunities for entertainment and culture within the boundaries of your new home.

As a career explorer, the job title you are currently seeking is like your familiar neighborhood. You'll explore all the possibilities within your "career city"—those that are connected with what you want to do—by examining your interests and skills and potential industries. After your exploration, you'll have a variety of new opportunities to pursue.

Interests and Skills

The best careers combine what we do well and what we like to do. Often, our interests and skills overlap—we're *good at* the things we *like* to do. However, our natural talents don't always match our interests.

To increase your career possibilities, leave no stone unturned when recording your skills and interests. A comprehensive list should consider:

- ❑ Every job you've ever had, even if it doesn't relate to the occupation you are currently seeking

- ❑ Every aspect of your working experience, including any secondary responsibilities that you did well and/or enjoyed doing

- ❑ Volunteer experiences

- ❑ Community activities

- ❑ Clubs or associations

- ❑ Classes or areas of study

- ❑ Hobbies

Each of these experiences can provide examples of your skills, interests, responsibilities, growth, priorities, dedication, and attitude. All of these elements are relevant to your job search and will be helpful to you when you prepare your resume.

Translating Interests into Job Skills

When you explore things you like to do in your free time, be sure to translate each of your interests into a possible job skill. For example, if one of your hobbies is making elaborate family tree albums for your friends and relatives, translate that interest into another job skill, such as *library and Internet research, art and composition,* or *product design.*

ETHICS & ETIQUETTE

It is unethical to misrepresent your experience to a potential employer. Be sure to list interests as skills *only* when you have actually performed the task.

For example, our model job seeker, Jamal, has attended many horse shows, but he has never worked at a stable. His experience is limited; therefore, he can use horse stables as a possible industry—but not a skill. Skill requires experience.

Of course, not everything you like to do or do well can be turned into a job skill. Any strong interest that cannot be turned into a job skill can usually be applied to your specific field of employment—the **industry** you work in—or your job title. For example, if you are an accountant and spend most of your free time rebuilding classic cars, it might be tough to convince an employer how this might benefit his or her operations. You could, however, work as an accountant for a car dealer, service center, or auto manufacturer.

Activity 2.1: Translation of Interests to Skills and Industries

Model Translation

Interest	Skill	Industry
Managing high school and college theater productions	Project and activity coordination and management	Dog shows
Walking the neighborhood dogs		Dog walking and boarding
Reading true-crime books	Analytical thinking	Police force; private investigation
Taking zoology classes and reading zoology books	Reading scientific and technical material	Animal research or zoological parks
Preparing dogs for Frisbee competitions		Dog training
Going to horse shows and competitions		Horse stables
Developing a classification system for a collection of 2,000 rocks	Devising organizational systems	Geology
Watching films with famous dogs		Movie dog training

Your Translation

Interest	Skill	Industry

Tips from the Pros

by Jennifer Floren
CEO and Founder, Experience.com, Inc.
(www.experience.com)

Top Five Tips for College Graduate Job Seekers

1. Employers' top complaint when interviewing students is that only 10% of the candidates interviewing for a job are prepared to answer the question: "Why do you want to work here?" Make sure you are among that 10%!

2. Unless you are completing a specific vocational or technical degree, your major will almost certainly NOT be a predictor of your career path. Focus your career development around your skills, interests, and aptitudes, not just on what you studied in school.

3. Your first job will not be your last! People in their 20s change jobs every 1.5 years *on average*...so go into your job search knowing that your first job is just the first stop on a long and exciting journey.

4. Pick your job based on what you think you will learn, and from whom. The top predictor of company loyalty is the relationship an employee has with his or her boss. Make sure you choose wisely, as the people around you will play an important role in shaping your future.

5. There is a very direct, proven correlation between career success and one's passion for the job. Keep that in mind: If you choose to do something that doesn't really excite and engage your enthusiasm, you risk being both unhappy *and* unsuccessful.

Jennifer Floren is the CEO and founder of Experience.com, Inc., the leading provider of career networks for colleges, universities, and employers seeking to hire educated talent. She has been recognized by *Working Woman, Boston Business Journal, Women's Business,* and *Entrepreneur* as one of the nation's youngest business leaders and achievers.

© 2002. Used with permission of the author.

Transferable Skills and Specialty Skills

Job skills are more than the abilities that specifically relate to their job titles or occupations, such as *network administration* or *medical transcription*. The skills that relate only to a specific profession or industry are your **specialty skills**. Though specialty skills are essential for expertise in any occupation, **transferable skills**—general skills that are valuable in most industries—can be moved from job field to job field.

Examples of Transferable Skills	**Examples of Specialty Skills**
Creative thinking	Desktop publishing
Problem solving	Computer programming
Communication skills	Machine repair

Because work environments change constantly, your employer might call on you to take on roles that don't match your particular job description. For instance, a computer programmer with excellent communication and teamwork skills might be asked to help train newer workers. Transferable skills make employees highly attractive to employers. Be sure to include them when you create your list of skills.

Activity 2.2: Skills List

It's time to create your list of skills. Jamal, who's looking for work as a veterinary technician, has listed his skills to guide you. Remember to list your interests as specialty skills or transferable skills. Though you'll want to list as many skills from your work experience as possible (at least 10), be sure to focus primarily on the work skills that you like *and* do well.

Model List

Specialty Skills	Transferable Skills
Organizing patient flow and schedules	Organizational skills
Following up with owners after a procedure	Crisis intervention and management
Handling incoming emergency patient calls	Helping others; customer service
Observing animals' health and adjusting feeding schedules accordingly	Analytical skills; problem solving
Cleaning cages and filling water bowls	Property maintenance and care
Exercising and playing with animals	Physical fitness; compassion
Checking animals for health problems and contacting the veterinarian if necessary	Recognizing symptoms
Reassuring owners that animals are well	Interpersonal skills
Coordinating jobs and tasks	Project management
Providing owners with dog obedience training	Teaching

Your List

Specialty Skills	Transferable Skills

Industries

Most job seekers will tell you that they don't care about what kind of industry they work in. One of the best ways to increase your career possibilities—*and* include your personal interests—is to open yourself up to a variety of industries. Don't limit yourself to one single industry. For instance, an administrative assistant could work in public education, city government, office supply distribution, magazine publishing, textile manufacturing, municipal utilities, travel and tourism, and medical fields.

5 STAR WEB SITES

For a comprehensive guide to industry and occupation names, visit the U.S. Department of Labor's *Career Guide to Industries* at **www.bls.gov/oco/cg/home.htm**

Activity 2.3: Industry List

It's time to create your list of desired industries. You can make your list as general or as specific as you like. For example, you might list food preparation and manufacturing as an industry, or you might want to be more specific and list gourmet food preparation. You should list at least 10 possible industries, but no more than 30.

Model List

- ❐ Veterinary care hospitals and clinics
- ❐ Boarding kennels
- ❐ Animal shelters
- ❐ Horse stables
- ❐ Animal research laboratories
- ❐ Animal obedience training schools

- ❐ Seeing-eye dog training schools
- ❐ Police dog training schools
- ❐ Movie dog training
- ❐ Zoological parks
- ❐ Dog show organizations and venues
- ❐ Geology

Your List

☐   ☐

☐   ☐

☐   ☐

☐   ☐

☐   ☐

☐   ☐

☐   ☐

☐   ☐

☐   ☐

☐   ☐

☐   ☐

☐   ☐

☐   ☐

☐   ☐

☐   ☐

Create Your Career Possibilities List

You're now ready to combine your list of skills and list of industries into a list of possible careers. To maximize your results, brainstorm alone or with a partner. Brainstorming is a strategy for setting our imaginations free to think of all possible avenues, no matter how unusual they might seem at the time. Though brainstorming is essentially a freethinking activity, follow the guidelines below for the best results.

☐ Produce as many ideas as possible.

☐ Write down every possible idea.

☐ Play "piggyback." Build on top of new ideas.

Activity 2.4: Career Possibilities List

For this activity, you'll need a sheet of paper. Begin by dividing the paper into two columns. Label one column *Possible Job Titles* and the other *Possible Career Options*. Then, using Jamal's model list as an example, list your possible job titles or occupations based on your education, your experience, and your skills list. Finally, combine the job titles with your list of industries to create a list of your possible careers. (For help with job titles and responsibilities, be sure to visit the Occupational Outlook Handbook at **www.bls.gov/oco/**).

Model List

Possible Job Titles	Possible Career Options
• Veterinary technician	• Veterinary technician in a hospital or clinic • Veterinary technician in an animal shelter • Veterinary technician in a kennel • Veterinary technician in a horse stable • Veterinary technician in a zoological park
• Dog trainer	• Dog trainer for police K-9 units • Dog trainer for seeing-eye dog schools • Dog trainer for obedience schools • Dog trainer for movies
• Animal care and service specialist	• Animal care and service specialist for a zoological park • Animal care and service specialist for a kennel • Animal care and service specialist for a research laboratory
• Research assistant	• Research assistant for a research laboratory
• Dog walker/exerciser	• Dog walker for a kennel
• Animal event coordinator	• Event coordinator for dog shows • Event coordinator for canine Frisbee championships

Checkpoint

1. Explain the difference between specialty and transferable skills. Why do you need both?

_____

_____

_____

_____

_____

2. List at least two new career opportunities from your career possibilities list. Did you discover these opportunities from your exploration of skills, interests, or industries? Explain.

_____

_____

_____

_____

Prioritizing Your Career Possibilities

At this point, your list of career options may seem overwhelming. Identifying your desired location, ideal work environment, and salary requirements will help you prioritize your career options and eliminate choices that don't suit you.

It is important to keep your original comprehensive career possibilities list. You may want to revisit it throughout your Internet job search.

Location, Location, Location

Knowing *where* you want to work is typically the easiest part of the career self-assessment process. If location is important to you, it can be one of the most important factors in refining your career possibilities search. It's not practical, for example, to look for work as a movie casting director if you must live near your small-town home in Maine.

Even if your career aspirations are more important to you than where you live, you still may have some issues to consider.

❑ Large cities have more job opportunities but higher costs of living. Could you live in New York, Chicago, Atlanta, or Los Angeles?

❑ Does city culture matter to you? Would you prefer an older city with a rich history, such as Boston, or a younger, booming city, such as Portland, Oregon?

❑ Do climate and region matter to you? Could you live on the coast? In the mountains? In extreme cold? Do you prefer a change in seasons?

Activity 2.5: Ideal Locations

Identify and prioritize your location requirements. (Your list may only have one location.) Use Jamal's list as an example.

Model Ideal Locations
1. Madison, Wisconsin
2. St. Paul, Minnesota
3. Portland, Oregon

Your Ideal Locations
1.

2.

3.

4.

Feeling at Home in Your Workplace

Don't underestimate the importance of your **work environment**, the "feel" of your workplace. It can make the difference between a successful and an unsuccessful career. What is a work environment? It's a difficult concept to put into words, because it encompasses many different factors, including:

- ❒ Setting (indoor vs. outdoor, office vs. factory)
- ❒ Dress requirements (formal vs. casual)
- ❒ Relationships with coworkers and supervisors (professional vs. friendly)
- ❒ Coworkers' personalities (idealistic, creative, introverted, etc.)
- ❒ Work pace (laid-back vs. high-energy)

An Ideal Work Environment

What is an ideal work environment? An ideal work environment gives you satisfaction and fulfillment and makes you feel happy to go to work each day. Though that definition is probably obvious to most of us, it can be difficult to pinpoint the characteristics that make a work environment ideal. Personal preferences may differ slightly, but most people look for the following qualities in a workplace.

- ❒ Recognition of accomplishments
- ❒ Opportunities for growth and promotion
- ❒ Surroundings that promote personal comfort
- ❒ Encouragement of creativity and resourcefulness
- ❒ Cultivation of open communication

Organization Size

When choosing your ideal work environment, you'll also want to consider the size of the organization. It is important to note that the following descriptions are general and may not apply to individual organizations. Though you can use the descriptions as a guide, part of your Internet job search will involve researching individual companies to learn more about what they have to offer.

- ❒ **Large organizations** (more than 1,000 employees) usually offer a stable company ideology. Some view them as impersonal, while others enjoy "blending with the crowd." Job responsibilities in large corporations are often strictly defined. Some workers enjoy having boundaries, while others don't feel comfortable with such limitations.

STATS

According to a 2001 study from the National Sleep Foundation, Americans work an average of 30% of their waking hours per week, and 38% of Americans work nearly 50% of their waking hours per week!

- ❑ **Mid-sized organizations** (100 to 1,000 employees) are often growing or are in a state of transition regarding products, services, or markets. This can provide a welcomed opportunity for change and advancement for some, while making others feel "lost." Many workers enjoy meeting people from different departments while still casually interacting with many of their coworkers and executive managers.

- ❑ **Small organizations** (fewer than 100 employees) typically promote a family-type environment, where everyone knows everyone. They facilitate casual communication between employees and managers and often allow employees to learn a variety of skills. Though job responsibilities are usually flexible, some workers find small companies to be socially and professionally limiting.

Activity 2.6: Ideal Work Environment

Think of at least five descriptive phrases that express the qualities of your ideal work environment, and prioritize them according to what is most important to you. Then prioritize your company size preference. (You do not need to include each type.) Use Jamal's sample as a guide.

Model Ideal Work Environment
1. Shows pride in producing highest-quality products or services
2. Values creativity and initiative
3. Casual dress and attitude
4. Open, supportive communication
5. Clear mission and purpose
6. Clearly defined job responsibilities
7. Values and practices organization and efficiency

Company size preference: 1. Mid-sized company
2. Small company
3. Large company

Your Ideal Work Environment
1.

2.

3.

4.

5.

Company size preference: 1.

2.

3.

Your Salary

All job seekers should have an idea of not only how much money they want to earn—their desired **salary**—but also what others earn in comparable careers and locations. Do you know the salary range for the position you are looking for in your desired location? Many people are surprised to find that they earn much less than the average salary range for their career and location. Regardless of whether making a lot of money is important to you, it helps to know what others in similar positions make.

You should also be aware of what benefits you require (or desire). Common benefits offered by employers are medical insurance, paid vacation days, flexible working hours, and pension plans. Consider a position's **compensation**, the combination of the salary and benefits—not just its salary—when comparing it to an average range.

Before you estimate your desired compensation range, ask yourself the following questions.

- ☐ Is making a lot of money important to me? Would I sacrifice other career desires to make more money?

- ☐ Am I willing to accept the challenges that typically go hand-in-hand with a larger salary (e.g., longer hours or more responsibility)?

- ☐ What benefits do I need and/or want?

- ☐ How much money do I need and/or want?

- ☐ How much money would I need in other locations?

5 STAR WEB SITES

Two well-known providers of salary calculators are **www.salary.com** and **www.homefair.com**.

Input information about your position and location and receive results listing the high, low, and median salaries for your career. (Other reports are available for a fee.) For an even more accurate picture, compare this information with the earnings information available from the Bureau of Labor Statistics at **www.bls.gov/oco**.

Try not to rely solely on online calculators for salary information. They are designed to provide only an approximate range for certain types of jobs. Before you demand a salary from an employer, make sure you have a clear understanding of the cost of living, the level of the position, experience required, and the other benefits that make up the compensation package. If you ask for too much, you could price yourself right out of a job.

Activity 2.7: Ideal Salary Range

Identify your salary requirements for each of your target locations. You may list your salary as a range if you like.

Model Desired Salary
1. Madison, Wisconsin: $25,000 to $30,000
2. St. Paul, Minnesota: $35,000 to $40,000
3. Portland, Oregon: $30,000 to $35,000

Your Desired Salary
1.

2.

3.

4.

Determining Your Career Values

Before you narrow down your options from your career possibilities list, determine what you value most about your career. Is salary (or compensation) more important than work environment? Is location more important than company size? Think about these questions as you complete Activity 2.8.

Activity 2.8: Career Value Table

For each career value below, assign a number that reflects its importance to you as a percentage of the whole career picture. For example, if salary is relatively unimportant to you, you'll want to give it a low number, such as 10 or 15. If you *must* work for a small company, assign work environment a high number, such as 50 or 60. The numbers you assign should be:

- ❑ Divisible by five (5, 10, 15, 20, etc.)
- ❑ **Equal to 100 when totaled**

Model Career Value Table

Jamal's highest priority is to work in Madison, Wisconsin. Work environment is relatively important to him, and he cares least about salary.

Career Value	Importance
Location	50
Work Environment	40
Salary	10
Total	100

Your Career Value Table

Career Value	Importance
Location	
Work Environment	
Salary	
Total	100

Using Career Values to Assess Career Options

Remember the exhaustive list of career options you created from your career possibilities list? Well, it's time to use your location, work environment, and salary assessments to shorten that list to a more manageable size. Your goal is to determine which careers have the characteristics you value—in other words, which careers are your ideal careers. Activity 2.9, which consists of three parts, will steer you through the process of creating a **career target list**. This prioritized list of career possibilities will be an important guide for finding your best job opportunities on the Internet.

Activity 2.9: Career Target List

This activity consists of three exercises.

    A. Career Options List
    B. Decision Tables
    C. Career Target List

Use Jamal's example as a guide for each exercise. You must complete all three parts in order to create a useful career target list. The more accurate and personalized your list is, the easier your Internet job search will be.

Exercise A: Career Options List

For this exercise, you'll want to choose four career options from the right column of your career possibilities list—the *Possible Career Options* column. Choose the four options that are the *least* alike. The order of your career options is not important. Use Jamal's list as an example.

Model Career Options List
1. Veterinary technician in a veterinary hospital or veterinary clinic
2. Dog trainer for obedience schools
3. Research assistant for an animal research laboratory

Your Career Options List
1.

2.

3.

4.

Exercise B: Decision Tables

For each career option, follow these steps to make a decision table.

1. Assign a number (on a scale from 5 to 100) to each career value that rates how well it is supported by the career option. 100 means it is ideal; 5 means it is unacceptable. Unlike in Activity 2.8, numbers do not need to total 100, but they should be divisible by 5.
2. Multiply the number in the *Importance* column by the number in the *How Well Career Option Supports Career Value* column to get a new total for each career value.
3. Add each new total to get a career score for each career option.

Model Decision Tables

Career Option 1 (Veterinary technician in a hospital or clinic)

Career Value	Importance		How Well Career Option Supports Career Value		Total
Location	50	×	50	=	2,500
Work Environment	40	×	70	=	2,800
Salary	10	×	40	=	400
			Career Score	=	5,700

Career Option 2 (Dog trainer for obedience schools)

Career Value	Importance		How Well Career Option Supports Career Value		Total
Location	50	×	50	=	2,500
Work Environment	40	×	90	=	3,600
Salary	10	×	30	=	300
			Career Score	=	6,400

Career Option 3 (Research assistant for an animal research laboratory)

Career Value	Importance		How Well Career Option Supports Career Value		Total
Location	50	×	90	=	4,500
Work Environment	40	×	5	=	200
Salary	10	×	80	=	800
			Career Score	=	5,500

Before Jamal performed a career self-assessment, he was looking for work only as a veterinary technician. But he discovered that his score for dog trainer is much higher than his score for veterinary technician. This doesn't mean Jamal should stop looking for work as a veterinary technician. It simply means he should prioritize dog training positions when searching for opportunities.

Your Decision Tables

Following the steps on the previous page and using Jamal's sample tables as a guide, fill in your decision tables—one for each of the four career options you chose in Exercise A. Feel free to use a calculator; you'll want your scores to be accurate.

Career Option 1 (_____)

Career Value	Importance		How Well Career Option Supports Career Value		Total
Location		×		=	
Work Environment		×		=	
Salary		×		=	
				Career Score =	

Career Option 2 (_____)

Career Value	Importance		How Well Career Option Supports Career Value		Total
Location		×		=	
Work Environment		×		=	
Salary		×		=	
				Career Score =	

Career Option 3 (_____)

Career Value	Importance		How Well Career Option Supports Career Value		Total
Location		×		=	
Work Environment		×		=	
Salary		×		=	
				Career Score =	

Career Option 4 (_____)

Career Value	Importance		How Well Career Option Supports Career Value		Total
Location		×		=	
Work Environment		×		=	
Salary		×		=	
				Career Score =	

Exercise C: Career Target List

Choose the top three career scores from your decision tables. These career options will make up your career target list—an invaluable guide for focusing your Internet job search.

Model Career Target List

1. Dog trainer for obedience schools
2. Veterinary technician in a hospital or clinic
3. Research assistant for an animal research laboratory

Your Career Target List

1.

2.

3.

Tips from the Pros

by Samer Hamadeh
President and CEO, Vault Inc. (www.vault.com)

Understanding company culture is key to job success. Too many people accept a job offer without knowing what their new employer really does, what the work environment is like, what employees think about the company, and whether the new employer and job are truly suited to their personality. You should always do your research—talk to current employees and ex-employees, ask interns, surf the company's Web site, and check out Vault's message boards and books—before you accept a job. By doing the research before you accept the job, you will be a more educated employee with a reduced learning curve. You may also save yourself from the aggravation and disappointment commonly associated with job dissatisfaction. It is a worthwhile investment of your time.

Samer Hamadeh is president and CEO of Vault Inc., the leading media company focused on careers, with a Web site, books, a syndicated newspaper column, and a personalized resume review and career coaching service. He co-founded Vault with Mark Oldman and Hussam Hamadeh in 1996.

 ## Checkpoint

1. Using your own experience, list some pros and cons of working in a large, mid-sized, or small company. Share your list with other members of your class.

   _____

   _____

2. Why should you research the salary range by location in your career field?

   _____

   _____

Internet Job Sites: A First Look

If you've never looked at Internet job listings, it's time to get your feet wet! In this exercise, you'll use your career target list as a guide for focusing your search. At this point, you won't be *applying* to online job listings—you'll do that after you create your resumes and cover letters.

For each category below, look at either *one* or *two* sites, depending on your career target list. For example, because location is his first priority, Jamal will want to look at *two* company Web sites in his location. He will only want to look at *one* online newspaper (the one in Madison, Wisconsin).

Job Boards and Career Sites

Job boards are Web sites that contain a searchable database of job openings from many different employers. **Career sites** offer advice about searching and applying for job openings. Most career sites also have job boards, and vice versa. Four of the most popular job boards/career sites follow. Some of them will ask you to set up an account (a username and a password). Try to use the same username and password throughout your Internet job search, and remember to *write them down*!

- ❏ America's Job Bank: **www.jobsearch.org**
- ❏ HotJobs®: **www.hotjobs.com**
- ❏ Monster®: **www.monster.com**
- ❏ CareerBuilder®: **www.careerbuilder.com**

Corporate Sites

A **corporate site** is an informational Web site for a particular company that sometimes offers information about the company's job openings. You may want to research corporate sites in your preferred location(s). If you don't know the URL for a company site, use a search engine—such as Google™ (**www.google.com**) or AltaVista® (**www.altavista.com**)—and enter the company's name. Not all company sites list job openings, but most do. Look for a heading such as *Careers* or *Employment*.

Online Newspapers

Most newspapers offer an online version—an **online newspaper**—that includes classified job openings. If you don't know the name of the newspaper you're looking for, try OnlineNewspapers.com (**www.onlinenewspapers.com**) for a comprehensive list of newspapers around the world that can be searched alphabetically or by region.

Industry, Nonprofit Career, and Government Career Sites

Industry sites offer information about careers and job openings for specific fields of employment. **Nonprofit career sites** list job openings for various nonprofit industries. **Government career sites** list openings for various branches of the government. Using your career target list as a guide, choose one or two Web sites from any of these categories. For example, if industry is important to you, use a search engine to find industry-specific listings (e.g., bookkeeping jobs). Or, if your work environment is a priority, you might want to search for online nonprofit listings at Idealist (**www.idealist.org**) or government listings at USAJOBS (**www.usajobs.opm.gov**) or Careers in Government (**www.careersingovernment.com**).

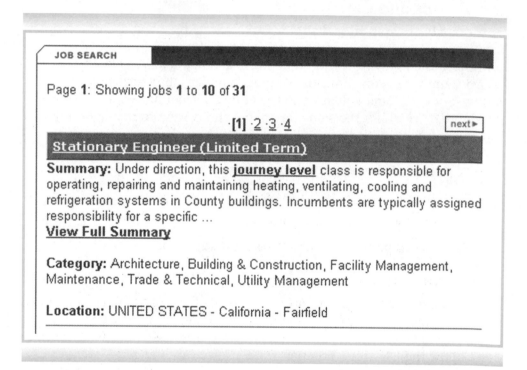

Figure 2.2 Government Career Site Job Listing
© 2002 CareersInGovernment.com. Reprinted by permission.

Checkpoint

List the three best job openings you found. How and where did you find them?

_____

_____

_____

_____

_____

_____

It's a Wrap

- ❏ One of the most common—and dangerous—mistakes job seekers make is beginning a job search without having a clear idea of what they're looking for.

- ❏ Finding a satisfying career involves a serious evaluation of your work experience, talents, and career values—or what career experts commonly call a career self-assessment.

- ❏ The best careers combine what we do well and what we like to do. Find these careers by examining your interests and skills and potential industries.

- ❏ Identifying your desired location, ideal work environment, and salary requirements will help you prioritize your career options and eliminate choices that don't suit you.

- ❏ Using your career target list as a guide will help you focus your Internet job search.

Learn the Lingo

Match each term to its definition.

Terms

___	**1.**	career site	___ **10.**	mid-sized organization
___	**2.**	career target list	___ **11.**	nonprofit career site
___	**3.**	compensation	___ **12.**	online newspaper
___	**4.**	corporate site	___ **13.**	salary
___	**5.**	government career site	___ **14.**	self-assessment
___	**6.**	industry	___ **15.**	small organization
___	**7.**	industry site	___ **16.**	specialty skills
___	**8.**	job board	___ **17.**	transferable skills
___	**9.**	large organization	___ **18.**	work environment

Definitions

- **a.** a Web site that offers career information and job openings for a specific field of employment
- **b.** general skills that are valuable regardless of the work environment or industry you work in
- **c.** the "feel" of a workplace; usually consists of the personalities of its employees, its level of formality, its setting, and its atmosphere
- **d.** a Web site that lists job openings for various nonprofit industries
- **e.** the total value of an employee's salary and benefits
- **f.** an evaluation, based on several personal elements, that is designed to help you know yourself
- **g.** a Web site that contains a searchable database of job openings
- **h.** a company with 100 to 1,000 employees

i. how much money an employee earns

j. a Web site for a particular company; often, but not always, offers information about the company's job openings

k. skills that relate to a specific profession or industry and cannot be transferred

l. a Web site that lists job openings for various branches of government

m. a prioritized list of careers that you might be suited for

n. a company with fewer than 100 employees

o. a Web site that offers advice about searching and applying for job openings

p. a specific field of employment

q. a company with more than 1,000 employees

r. an online version of a newspaper; usually includes classified job openings

E-valuation

1. Take two of the online self-assessments listed in the chapter, and then answer the questions below.

   a. How did the assessments differ? How were they similar?

   b. What did the assessments measure?

   c. Do you agree with the assessments' results? Why or why not?

   d. What aspect of your job search do the results apply to, if any? Explain.

2. Translate each of the interests below into a skill or an industry.

   a. Playing strategy board games, such as Risk or chess

   b. Reading entertainment magazines for information on celebrities

   c. Helping other students revise their term papers and essays

   d. Volunteering at Special Olympics games and events

3. Go to **www.salary.com**. For each career on your career target list, determine the average salary in your first-choice location. Are you surprised by the results? Why or why not?

4. Did you find the process involved in creating your career target list (Activity 2.9) useful? If so, explain how it was useful. If not, what factors would you have included or excluded to make your results more accurate?

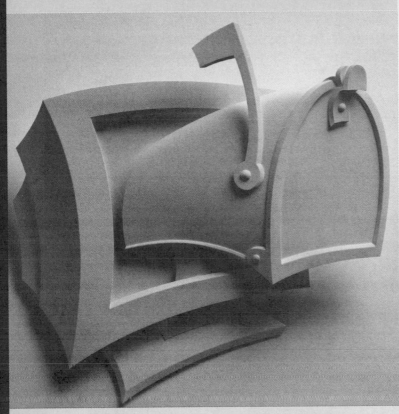

CHAPTER OBJECTIVES

❐ Discover the types of resumes used in Internet job searches, and learn when to use them.

❐ Understand the standard elements of successful resumes.

❐ Use keywords effectively in your resumes.

❐ Create your Internet-ready resumes.

❐ Create your Internet-ready cover letters.

CREATING RESUMES AND COVER LETTERS

CHAPTER 3

"Pounding the pavement" is a perfect description of what traditional job searches were like prior to the Internet. Savvy job seekers literally covered miles of pavement, visiting several prospective employers with their fancy paper resumes in tow. As an Internet job seeker, you'll be pounding the *virtual* pavement—the information superhighway—and the rules of the road have changed. Though the traditional paper resume still plays a role, it will not be your only—or your most important—resume during your Internet job search.

Depending on the situation and the employer's request, you'll need to send different types of resumes throughout your Internet job search, including your traditional paper resume. In this chapter, you'll discover how easy it is to create every type of resume you'll need from *one* basic resume. You'll also discover which resume you should use in the different situations you'll encounter.

Model Job Seeker

Our model job seeker for this chapter is Marisa. She has an associate's degree in healthcare information technology and work experience as an office manager and an intern at a medical center. Marisa has recently passed the CPHIMS (Certified Professional in Healthcare Information and Management Services) and RHIT (Registered Health Information Technician) certification exams. Based on the career target list she created in Chapter 2, she has determined that she would like to pursue a career as a medical records technician in a hospital or large doctor's office. Marisa's resumes and cover letters are provided as examples throughout this chapter.

The New Resumes: Substance over Style

Companies and Internet job sites are using new technologies to make the process of searching for candidates more efficient. **Resumes** are documents that summarize candidates' education, work experience, and skills. These important documents are now routinely stored in resume databases, which can be searched by **keywords**—special words related to specific jobs and skills that are used to search computer databases. Unfortunately, most formatting features that are fundamental to standard paper resumes, such as columns and bullets, cannot be "understood" by resume databases. That's why computer-friendly resumes are taking center stage. And if you want to be a player on that stage, your resume should be dressed for the part.

How are computer-friendly resumes dressed for the part? They have less *style*—or formatting—so that computers can read them and more *substance*—or career-related keywords—so that company and job site databases can match skills to opportunities. Though formatted paper resumes are still used in today's job-seeking process, they often find themselves all dressed up with no place to go.

Three technologies have pushed the standard resume to the background.

- ❐ *Scanners:* Many organizations read resumes with computer scanners, which often cannot understand formatting elements such as boldface fonts, columns, and bullets.

- ❐ *E-mail:* Resumes are now routinely accepted as e-mail text or e-mail attachments. When an online job listing asks that resumes be attached to e-mail, unless otherwise specified, you should send a plain-text, or **ASCII** ("askie"), resume. In fact, many companies prefer to receive plain-text e-mailed resumes over any other resume format.

- ❐ *Resume-tracking software:* More and more organizations are putting these scanned and e-mailed resumes in resume-tracking databases, which use keyword searches to retrieve information from the resumes about candidates' specific skills and work experience.

Paper vs. Electronic Resumes

Before you look at the basic types of resumes you'll use in your Internet job search, it's important to understand the crucial difference between paper resumes and electronic resumes. Fortunately, the difference is simple—it relates to how you send or deliver your resume. **Paper resumes** are delivered in paper form, either through the postal service or in person. **Electronic resumes** are delivered electronically. They are e-mailed as a computer file, uploaded to a job board or company Web site, or "built" by pasting resume sections into online resume-builder fields. There is *no paper* involved in the transmission of electronic resumes.

NOW YOU KNOW

ASCII stands for American Standard Code for Information Interchange. It is a simple form of text that most computers can read and process. For example, a Word document can be saved as ASCII text by using the *Save As* command and selecting the type *text only*.

The Online Job Search Resume Types

Paper resumes and electronic resumes differ only by method of delivery. So, for all intents and purposes, an electronic resume becomes a paper resume when you print it on paper, and a paper resume becomes an electronic resume when you send it via e-mail or post it to a Web site. Converting your resumes is almost that easy, but not quite.

Paper Resumes

Though you may not know it (or like it), paper resumes are almost always scanned for entry into a resume database. That's why a **scannable resume**—one that is formatted to be read easily by a computer scanner—should be the default when sending paper resumes. However, sometimes an employer will specifically ask for a Word resume (a resume formatted with word processing software). When employers ask for your Word resume, they are referring to your traditional formatted paper resume, or what we'll be calling your **personalized resume**. Therefore, every job seeker should have two kinds of paper resumes.

- ❑ *A paper scannable resume:* This resume is formatted so that it can be understood by computer scanners.

- ❑ *A paper personalized resume:* This is your Word resume. It is formatted with columns, centering, boldface, italics, and/or any other graphic elements that illustrate your style and personality.

Electronic Resumes

Likewise, when employers and career Web sites receive electronic resumes via e-mail or through a Web site, they input them into resume-tracking databases. That's why a plain-text (or ASCII) resume should be the default when sending electronic resumes. However, sometimes an employer will specifically ask for your personalized resume. Therefore, every job seeker should have two kinds of electronic resumes.

- ❑ *An electronic plain-text resume:* This resume is formatted in plain text so that it can be understood by resume-tracking databases.

- ❑ *An electronic personalized resume:* This is your Word resume. It is formatted with columns, centering, boldface, italics, and/or any other graphic elements that illustrate your style and personality.

Your "default" resumes are the ones you'll use every time you apply to an online job posting, *unless* you are specifically asked to send a different resume format.

NOW YOU KNOW

If you feel a bit overwhelmed, don't worry! Two of the four resumes mentioned so far are actually the same resume. You'll use the same personalized resume for both paper and electronic purposes. There is only one small difference: When you send it as a paper resume, you'll print it on nice resume paper.

Web Resumes and Portfolios

The most important thing to know about a Web resume is that you don't necessarily need one. Though it may be formatted in plain text, a **Web resume** is typically an electronic personalized resume that you post to a personal Web site. Job seekers with Web resumes include the Web site's URL on their electronic plain-text resumes to direct employers to the site. Many job seekers also post their professional work on the same site in the form of a **Web portfolio**, which is an electronic collection of work samples that can demonstrate specific skills and talents, such as technical writing or photography. Though Web resumes and portfolios aren't necessary for the Internet job seeker, they project the technical and professional competence, initiative, and creativity that employers value.

Built Resumes

A **built resume** is not technically a different resume. It is simply a "pieced-together" version of your electronic plain-text resume. A **wizard**, or computer guide, can help you build your resume via simple steps.

Most career sites offer job seekers two ways of posting resumes.

- ❑ *A free-form upload procedure:* You copy and paste your entire electronic plain-text resume into a form, and your resume is uploaded to the Web site.

- ❑ *A resume wizard:* The wizard walks you through the process in a step-by-step fashion, asking you to input individual segments of your electronic plain-text resume into a template. The pieces are then compiled to create your resume.

The Order of Things: Resume Types by Use

Why will your Internet job search call for different resume types? Because companies and career Web sites will use your resume in different ways and for different reasons. One employer may ask you to send your resume via e-mail so it can be entered into a resume-tracking database. Another may specifically ask you to e-mail your personalized resume because the company is interested in seeing your formal, designed resume but does not want to wait for it to arrive through the postal service.

NOW YOU KNOW

While resume wizards are helpful guides, they cannot provide content or creativity. They can merely compile the information that you supply. For this reason, you must make sure the individual segments of your resume are clear, correct, and relevant.

Though your experience may vary slightly, the following order represents how often each resume type is used by the average Internet job seeker.

1. Electronic plain-text resume (used most)
2. Electronic personalized resume
3. Built resume
4. Paper scannable resume
5. Paper personalized resume
6. Web resume (used least)

Resume Formats at a Glance

Though we've introduced six different resumes, each resume type translates to one of only three resume formats that you'll need for your Internet job search; plain-text, scannable, and personalized. **Figure 3.1** shows how to translate resume types to resume formats.

Resume Type	Resume Format
Electronic plain-text resume	Plain-text (ASCII)
Built resume	
Web resume (sometimes)	
Paper scannable resume	Scannable
Paper personalized resume	Personalized
Electronic personalized resume	
Web resume (sometimes)	

Figure 3.1 Resume Types and Formats

Checkpoint

1. Which resume should be your default when sending electronic resumes? Why?

_____

_____

_____

_____

_____

2. Which resume should be your default when sending paper resumes? Why?

_____

_____

_____

_____

_____

Resume Basics

The fact that you're reading this book suggests that you probably already have one or more versions of a resume. If that's true, the information provided in this section will help you refine your resume for your Internet job search. If you don't have a resume, this section will guide you through the basic development process with ease.

To make the process of creating your resume simpler, you will create or revise only *one* resume. You will then reformat your resume into the three main resume formats: plain-text, scannable, and personalized.

Creating Your Personal Inventory

A personal inventory is a written statement of everything about you that may be interesting to a potential employer. Personal inventories can be especially useful when answering interview questions. They are also used to complete resumes, cover letters, and online job applications.

Activity 3.1: Personal Inventory

Use the personal inventory form on the next page (or create a new Word document) to prepare a record of your education, experience, skills, and interests. A sample from our model job seeker, Marisa, is provided to guide you.

Model Personal Inventory

Immediate Goal: A position as a medical records technician in a hospital or large doctor's office

Long-term Goal: A position as a medical records administrator or as a tumor registrar

Personal Characteristics: Organized, patient, detail-oriented, polite, helpful to customers, sensitive to patient privacy

Special Skills: ICD-9 coding, color-coded filing systems, accounts receivable and payable, AS400, QuickBooks, audits, contracts, orders, and vouchers, type 50 wpm, ten-key 200 spm

Work Experience:

Job 1: Doctor's office manager, June 2002 to present
Maintain records for patients; compile and produce reports for insurance records; handle accounts payable, accounts receivable, and payroll; use spreadsheet, data management, word processing, and Internet software programs

Job 2: Medical center intern, January 2001 to May 2002
Greeted and registered patients; scheduled appointments; assisted the bookkeeper with patient accounts

Education and Certification:

Degree: Associate of Applied Science, 2002, College of Applied Careers, Spokane, WA
Major: Healthcare Information Technology
Minor: Accounting
Certification: CPHIMS, RHIT

Activities and Volunteer Experiences: Served as a chaperone for seniors on assisted-living community field trips; volunteered as an office assistant at a local free clinic

References:

Dr. Jean Rafael, 106 Government Way, Coeur D'Alene, ID 83814

Dr. Raul Cortez, Community Medical Center, 1102 Sweetheart Lane, Coeur D'Alene, ID 83816

Your Personal Inventory

Immediate Goal:

Long-term Goal:

Personal Characteristics:

Special Skills:

Work Experience:

Education and Certification:

Activities and Volunteer Experiences:

References:

Multiple Resume Versions

Some job seekers like to use multiple resume versions that are targeted to specific careers. For example, Jamal, the model job seeker from Chapter 2, has somewhat dissimilar job types on his career target list— veterinary technician, dog trainer, and research assistant. Therefore, he might want to write different resume objectives or change the focus of his work experience when applying for different jobs.

Whether you'll use one or more versions of a resume, remember that each version of your resume will be formatted into the three main resume formats. So, if you have two versions of your resume, you'll have six total resumes.

Resume Styles: Chronological and Functional

The **chronological resume**, arranges work experience according to time sequence (most recent first) and is used to demonstrate steady, relevant work experience.

A **functional resume** focuses on skills, personal attributes, and any relevant volunteer or job experience. It highlights what you *can do*, instead of what you *have done*. Functional resumes focus on career-related skills and abilities, including any specific expertise, technical knowledge, and computer skills. They also incorporate personal attributes, such as leadership, organization, motivation, and cooperation.

When to Use a Chronological Resume

Employers tend to prefer this format. It should be used when you have a strong formal education and/or strong employment experience in your desired field. Use a chronological resume:

- ❐ When your work experience occupies the same field.
- ❐ When your job history shows real growth or advancement.
- ❐ When your prior job titles and companies are impressive.

When to Use a Functional Resume

If you're a first-time job seeker or have just been trained in your new vocation, you might be perplexed as to how you'll present your work experience in your resume. For example, you may have just earned your certification as a dental hygienist but prior to that worked as a daycare assistant. If you fall into this category, a functional resume is best for you. Use a functional resume:

- ❐ When you lack work experience directly related to your job target.
- ❐ When your skills are more impressive than your years on the job.
- ❐ When you've frequently changed careers or have gaps in employment.

Resume Sections

The following sections are ordered according to traditional standards. **See Figure 3.3** on page 53 for examples of resume sections.

☐ *Contact information:* At the top of your resume, provide your name; address; phone number; e-mail address; and additional information, such as a fax number or URL for your Web resume.

☐ *Objective:* State your desired job title(s) or type of work and the broad qualifications that you want to utilize. Some objectives include both short-term and long-term employment goals. A clear, appropriate job objective will focus your entire resume.

☐ *Summary of Qualifications and Skills:* List, in order of importance, your abilities and skills that are most relevant to the job you are seeking (your objective). This resume section is vital for the Internet job seeker and the most important section of a functional resume. Your summary of qualifications and skills should be packed with industry terms that will draw potential employers to your resume. Be sure to include specific expertise, technical knowledge, computer skills, and specialized certifications. You can emphasize your skills by breaking this section into separate labeled paragraphs, such as *Computer Skills* and *Management Skills*. In each paragraph, clearly identify your skill that relates to the job objective. State measurable accomplishments, such as, "Text input at 75 wpm," or "Increased regional sales 25%."

☐ *Education:* In reverse chronological order, list the names and locations of the school(s) you've attended and any diploma(s), degree(s), certificates, or honors you've received. You may also include your major, minor, or a list of related courses. If your GPA was high, include it on your resume.

☐ *Work experience:* List your most recent work (or military) experience first. Include the name and location of each company, dates of employment, and a brief, results-oriented description of your job. This is the most important section of a chronological resume, and your descriptions should stress your major responsibilities and measurable accomplishments in each position.

☐ *Additional experience:* List any volunteer activities, organization memberships, and leadership roles that relate to your career objectives and/or would impress a future employer. (This section is optional.)

☐ *References:* Employers expect *all* applicants to have references but differ regarding when and where they want to see an applicant's reference list. It is acceptable, but not necessary, to end your resume with the standard phrase, "References available upon request."

NOW YOU KNOW

Recruiters want to see objective statements that match the position you're applying for. If you have differing target careers, you'll want to have a few resume versions that have different objectives. Never write a vague objective—it leads recruiters to believe that you don't know what you want.

ETHICS & ETIQUETTE

Before you use work contacts as references, *always* ask them for permission first. You also might want to tell them what kind of work you're looking for so that they can talk intelligently about what you will bring to the new position.

There is, however, some room for variation from this standard order. Because some resume-building wizards have a limit of 100 to 250 words, you may want to put keyword-packed sections, such as your summary of qualifications, before your objective. Some job seekers switch the order of their education and work experience to place education last. If your education is impressive (advanced degrees, top-notch schools, or outstanding grades), you might want to place it before your work experience. Job seekers who use a functional resume format but include a brief work experience section may want to place their work experience last, depending on how well the experience matches the position sought.

A Resume Worth Doing is Worth Doing Well

Potential employers try to reduce large stacks of resumes by quickly eliminating those that don't meet their needs. If your resume is poorly written, has typos, or doesn't conform to standard resume length, it won't make the cut. Practice the following guidelines to ensure your resume makes it past the first elimination round.

- ❏ *Use correct spelling and grammar.* Proofread your resume carefully. Use your word processor's spell checker, but don't rely on it solely. Spell checkers don't catch every typo, and grammar checkers are often inaccurate. Always have someone else read your resume to catch errors. Misspelled words, typing mistakes, and formatting errors are flaws that can cause your resume to be rejected.

- ❏ *Be clear and specific.* Use clear, concise, professional language. Provide specific examples that use numbers (such as percentage increases) and action verbs to describe your accomplishments. A thesaurus can help you use the best words to describe your capabilities.

- ❏ *Be brief.* A resume from a job seeker who has been in the workforce for fewer than three years should not exceed one page. More experienced job applicants should keep resumes to one or two pages.

 **Checkpoint**

1. Explain the difference between resume versions and resume formats.

   _____

   _____

2. Why is the summary of qualifications section so important to Internet job seekers?

   _____

   _____

Using Keywords to Your Advantage

Career sites and individual companies store resumes in databases to ease the job-candidate matchmaking process. For example, a human resources manager of a firm with 3,000 employees may have 100 to 250 jobs available at any given time. To narrow down the candidates for the openings, he or she would need to read between 2,500 and 25,000 resumes. The numbers are even more staggering for e-recruiters: Job boards carry hundreds of thousands—even millions—of resumes. In these circumstances, narrowing down potential matches for a position would require an excessive amount of people hours. That's why it has become a job for computers.

NOW YOU KNOW

Think of your computer-friendly resume as a keyword catalog that represents your skills and experience.

If you're applying for jobs through the career sites or through the Web sites of large or mid-sized companies (even small companies are beginning to use resume-tracking software), you must understand that a computer will "read" your resume before it reaches human hands. When a computer reads your resume, it is looking for career-related keywords in the text of your resume sections.

Understanding Matching Technology

Whenever technology is involved in a process of selection or matching, a formula or set of rules is involved. The technology used for resume databases utilizes a search-matching function—a set of rules that allows a search result to be displayed based on the input given by the user (a recruiter, for example).

In most cases, the search technology used for career sites is based on **keyword searches** (searches for specific words or phrases) and **Boolean searches** (searches that include logical operators, such as *AND*, *OR*, and *NOT*). How does it work?

- ❒ Results are displayed based on the occurrences of matching search terms, or resume keywords.

- ❒ Resumes with more matches are placed higher on the results list.

- ❒ Though results are generally displayed based on relevancy of the keyword matching, some career sites may have additional methods for prioritizing candidates, such as when you posted your resume, your geographic area, or your salary requirement.

It's important to remember that computer-friendly resumes, such as your electronic plain-text resume, differ from your traditional (personalized) resume in two ways.

Computer-friendly resumes have:

- ❒ *Less "style."* The fancy formatting, such as a special font, is removed so that resume databases and computer scanners can read them.

❐ *More "substance."* They are packed with career-related keywords so that they get more "hits" when computers search them.

What Types of Keywords do Recruiters Look For?

NOW YOU KNOW

If you are applying for a position that lists many required skills, your resume must demonstrate proficiency in each requirement.

When recruiters search resume databases for keywords or keyword phrases (more than one keyword in a string, such as *database administration*), they are typically looking for words that are:

❐ *Nouns.* When a computer searches your resume for keywords, it will not be looking for verbs! Though you can still use action verbs (*managed, trained, researched*) to describe your work experience, if the experience you're describing is part of your target career job title, you'll get more matches if you rephrase your experience. For example, a software trainer will want to say "acted as *software trainer* for tri-state area," instead of "*trained* all new software users in tri-state area."

❐ *Career-related.* Be sure to include keywords that are specific to your industry, job skills, and job title. Visualize yourself as the employer. What would you want to know about someone applying for a job in your field? Include position titles, career-specific certifications, computer programs and programming languages, and other specific skills. Use appropriate, well-known abbreviations, such as *RN*. These are the same terms that are used in job descriptions and job ads.

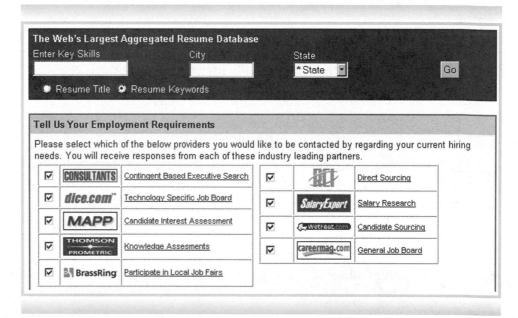

Figure 3.2 Employer Resume Search Fields
© 2002 Entrepreneur.com, Inc. Reprinted by permission.

Writing Your Keyword Summary

The easiest way to pack your resume with career-related keywords is to include as many keywords as you can in your summary of qualifications. Call this section *Summary of Qualifications*, *Summary of Skills*, *Skills Summary*, *Related Capabilities*, or something similar.

Activity 3.2: Keyword Summary

Use the space below to create your keyword summary. Use similar categories to the ones Marisa used, or create your own. (Your keyword summary does not need to be separated with headings.) You will use this summary to build the Summary of Qualifications section of your resume.

Model Keyword Summary

Medical records management: ICD-9 coding, color-coded filing systems
Certification: CPHIMS and RHIT
Computer programs: AS400 and QuickBooks
Financial management: A/R, A/P, audits, contracts, orders, and vouchers

Your Keyword Summary

Checkpoint

1. In your own words, explain how recruiters use keywords to match potential candidates with job openings.

   _____

   _____

   _____

2. Write a list of keywords for one of the jobs you found in Chapter 2. What keywords are used in the ad? What other keywords might the employer look for?

   _____

   _____

   _____

Creating Your Resumes

If you've never written a resume, you'll find that the personal inventory you created in Activity 3.1 will serve as a basis for the content and the basic resume sections will serve as the structure. Don't forget to include keywords in your summary of qualifications and make keyword changes, if necessary, to your work experience.

Though computer-friendly resumes focus on career-related keywords and employ different formats, they still follow the basic resume principles. Your resume should identify the talents that apply to the career you're seeking. It should be simple, well-worded, and brief.

Creating Your Resume Sections

To create the basis for your resume, open a new word-processing document and type in your resume sections. Don't worry about formatting at this point. You'll reformat your resume into the three basic formats later in this section.

Your resume sections should be similar to the resume sections provided by Marisa in **Figure 3.3**. Note that she has decided to use the chronological style.

Formatting Your Electronic Plain-Text Resume

The main rule for formatting your electronic plain-text resume is to not use any formatting elements that cannot be found on your keyboard. The only exception to this rule is tabs. Though tabs appear on your keyboard, they confuse computers scanners. Therefore, all spacing should be made with hard returns or with your space bar.

Electronic plain-text resumes should *not* have:

- Bullets
- *Italics* or **boldface**
- Centering, full justification, or right justification. Use *only* left justification of text.
- Lines
- Columns
- Fancy fonts. Use only 10-point or 12-point Courier.
- Spaces made with tabs. Use only a hard return or your space bar to indent lines or make spaces between lines.
- Colors. Use only black text.

Resume Sections

Contact Information:
Marisa R. Georges
203 Apple Tree Lane
Coeur D'Alene, Idaho 83814
(208) 555-9087
Fax: (208) 555-6452
E-mail: mrgeorges@live.net

Objective:
Medical records technician position in a hospital or medical office where my health records experience will promote the accuracy, privacy, and convenience of patient records

Summary of Qualifications:
- Medical records management using ICD-9 coding and color-coded filing systems
- CPHIMS and RHIT certification
- Database design and maintenance using AS400
- Advanced spreadsheet generation and word processing with Excel and Word XP
- Text input at 50 wpm and ten-key by touch at 200 spm
- Financial management with QuickBooks, including A/R, A/P, audits, contracts, orders, and vouchers
- Proven commitment to customer service and patient privacy

Experience:
Dr. Jean Rafael, 106 Government Way, Coeur D'Alene, ID 83814
Office Manager, June 2002 to present
- Maintain records for all patients, including active and inactive files
- Implemented new system for producing reports for insurance records; reduced report generation time by 30%
- Handle accounts payable, accounts receivable, and payroll
- Use spreadsheet, database, word processing, and Internet software programs

Community Medical Center, 1102 Sweetheart Lane, Coeur D'Alene, ID 83816
Intern, January 2001 to May 2002
- Greeted and registered patients
- Answered the telephones and scheduled appointments
- Assisted the bookkeeper with patient accounts

Education:
Associate of Applied Science, 2002, College of Applied Careers, Spokane, WA
Major: Healthcare Information Technology
Minor: Accounting
Related Courses: Medical Terminology, Health Information Management, Clinical Classification, Health Law and Ethics, Financial Accounting, Cost Accounting
Certification: CPHIMS and RHIT

Figure 3.3 Model Resume Sections (chronological organization)

To format your electronic plain-text resume, follow these steps.

1. Open your resume sections document, and select and copy the text.

2. Open a new word-processing document, and paste the copied text. Your page size should be a standard 8½ × 11".

3. Reformat any elements that cannot be read by a computer database.

4. Set your margins for no more than 65 characters per line or a minimum of one-inch outside margins.

5. Save your document as a plain-text ("text only") file with a name that designates it as your plain-text resume. (At this point, your software program may warn you that you will lose formatting elements. That's OK—you don't want them!)

Marisa's electronic plain-text resume is shown in **Figure 3.4**. Plain, isn't it? It can be difficult to get used to, especially if you've been using personalized resumes for your job searches. There is no reason to feel uneasy, though. Everyone else's resume will be as plain as yours.

When to Use Your Electronic Plain-Text Resume
Your electronic plain-text resume will get the most use during your Internet job search. Unless an employer or career site *specifically* asks for a different type of resume, use your electronic plain-text resume when:

❒ An employer or contact asks you to e-mail a resume.

❒ Posting a resume to a career site database.

❒ E-mailing a resume to a company Web site.

❒ A job posting includes an e-mail address.

NOW YOU KNOW

Unless they specify otherwise, most companies will not accept e-mail attachments, which may be contaminated with viruses.

To avoid having your attachment rejected, paste your electronic plain-text resume into the body of your e-mail.

Marisa R. Georges
203 Apple Tree Lane
Coeur D'Alene, Idaho 83814
(208) 555-9087
Fax: (208) 555-6452
E-mail: mrgeorges@live.net

OBJECTIVE
Medical records technician position in a hospital or medical office
where my health records experience will promote the accuracy,
privacy, and convenience of patient records

SUMMARY OF SKILLS
Medical records management: ICD-9 coding and color-coded filing
systems; proven commitment to customer service and patient privacy
Certification: CPHIMS and RHIT
Computer programs: AS400 and QuickBooks
Financial management: A/R, A/P, audits, contracts, orders, vouchers

EXPERIENCE
Dr. Jean Rafael
106 Government Way, Coeur D'Alene, ID 83814
Office Manager, June 2002 to present
- Maintain records for all patients; active and inactive files
- Compile reports for insurance records; reduced report generation
  time by 30%
- Handle accounts payable, accounts receivable, and payroll
- Use spreadsheet, database management, word processing, and
Internet software programs

Community Medical Center
1102 Sweetheart Lane, Coeur D'Alene, ID 83816
Intern, January 2001 to May 2002
- Greeted and registered patients
- Answered the telephones and scheduled appointments
- Assisted the bookkeeper with patient accounts

EDUCATION
College of Applied Careers, Spokane, WA
Associate of Applied Science, 2002
Major: Healthcare Information Technology
Minor: Accounting
Related Courses: Medical Terminology, Health Information
Management, Clinical Classification, Health Law and Ethics,
Financial Accounting, Cost Accounting
Certification: CPHIMS and RHIT

Figure 3.4 Model Electronic Plain-Text Resume (shown at 75% actual size)

Formatting Your Paper Scannable Resume

The format of your paper scannable resume is similar to your electronic plain-text resume. However, unlike electronic plain-text resumes, paper scannable resumes:

☐ Use hyphens instead of parentheses around phone and fax number area codes—208-555-9087 instead of (208) 555-9087. Most scanners cannot read parentheses.

☐ Can use one simple, clean font such as Arial or Times Roman and font sizes of 10-14 points. For example, you can increase your contact information and heading fonts up to 14 points.

☐ Can use acceptable *basic* formatting such as boldface type, solid bullets, and tabs. Do not use italic formats or fancy typefaces.

☐ Must be printed in black ink only on white, high-quality 8½ × 11" paper—the whiter the better.

To format your paper scannable resume, follow these steps.

1. Open your electronic plain-text resume; select and copy the text.

2. Open a new document, and paste the copied text.

3. Save the new document as a word-processing document—not as plain-text—with a name that designates it as your paper scannable resume.

4. Set your margins for no more than 65 characters per line or a minimum of one-inch outside margins.

5. Change the font if necessary and enlarge contact information and headings for readability.

6. Replace parentheses around phone and fax numbers with hyphens.

7. If your resume is longer than one page, put your name and e-mail address or phone number at the top of the second page.

8. Print the resume in black ink on bright white 8½ × 11" paper.

When to Use Your Paper Scannable Resume

Your paper scannable resume is your default paper resume. Unless an employer or career site specifically asks for a personalized resume, use your paper scannable resume whenever an employer asks you to fax a resume and whenever you mail a paper resume to an employer.

How to Send Your Paper Scannable Resume

Paper scannable resumes are either faxed or sent through the mail. Do not fax your paper scannable resume unless asked to do so. Scanners do not read faxes as well as they read normal paper documents. When faxing, turn on the "fine print" feature of your fax machine. It will help the scanner read your resume. When mailing, do not fold or staple your resume. Marisa's paper scannable resume is shown in **Figure 3.5.**

Marisa R. Georges
203 Apple Tree Lane
Coeur D'Alene, Idaho 83814
208-555-9087
Fax: 208-555-6452
E-mail: mrgeorges@live.net

OBJECTIVE

Medical records technician position in a hospital or medical office where my health records experience will promote the accuracy, privacy, and convenience of patient records

SUMMARY OF SKILLS

Medical records management: ICD-9 coding and color-coded filing systems; proven commitment to customer service and patient privacy
Certification: CPHIMS and RHIT
Computer programs: AS400 and QuickBooks
Financial management: A/R, A/P, audits, contracts, orders, vouchers

EXPERIENCE
Dr. Jean Rafael

106 Government Way, Coeur D'Alene, ID 83814
Office Manager, June 2002 to present
- Maintain records for all patients; active and inactive files
- Compile reports for insurance records; reduced report generation time by 30%
- Handle accounts payable, accounts receivable, and payroll
- Use spreadsheet, database, word processing, and Internet software programs

Community Medical Center

1102 Sweetheart Lane, Coeur D'Alene, ID 83816
Intern, January 2001 to May 2002
- Greeted and registered patients
- Answered the telephones and scheduled appointments
- Assisted the bookkeeper with patient accounts

EDUCATION

College of Applied Careers, Spokane, WA
Associate of Applied Science, 2002
Major: Healthcare Information Technology
Minor: Accounting
Related Courses: Medical Terminology, Health Information Management, Clinical Classification, Health Law and Ethics, Financial Accounting, Cost Accounting
Certification: CPHIMS and RHIT

Figure 3.5 Model Paper Scannable Resume (shown at 75% actual size)

Formatting Your Personalized Resume

Personalized resumes allow employers to get a quick glimpse of candidates' personalities before they are called for interviews. Though they use graphic elements, personalized resumes should not be too busy, outlandish, or gaudy. Remember, you're trying to attract a broad range of people. For that reason, less is always more when personalizing your resume.

Personalized resumes can utilize:

- ❑ Bullets
- ❑ *Italics* and **boldface**
- ❑ Centering, full justification, right justification, and left justification
- ❑ Lines, shapes, and simple graphic elements
- ❑ Columns
- ❑ Fancier fonts. But be conservative. The main text should be between 10 points and 12 points in size, and the contact information and headings should not exceed 16 points.
- ❑ Spaces that are made with tabs

To format your personalized resume, follow these steps.

1. Open your electronic plain-text resume, and select and copy the text.

2. Open a new document, and paste the copied text.

3. Save the new document as a word-processing document with a name that designates it as your personalized resume.

4. Add your preferred formatting elements, such as centering, boldface, tabbed spaces, and bullets.

Marisa's personalized resume is shown in **Figure 3.6** on the next page.

When to Use Your Electronic Personalized Resume

You'll use your electronic personalized resume when an employer specifically asks you to e-mail a Word resume, or when posting your resume to a career site that specifically asks for a personalized resume.

When to Use and How to Send Your Paper Personalized Resume

You'll use your paper personalized resume only when an employer or recruiter specifically asks you to mail a copy of your Word resume. Print your resume in black ink on high-quality 8½ × 11" resume paper in a shade of white or beige. Send it in a matching envelope.

Marisa R. Georges

203 Apple Tree Lane
Coeur D'Alene, Idaho 83814
(208) 555-9087
Fax: (208) 555-6452
E-mail: mrgeorges@live.net

OBJECTIVE

Medical records technician position in a hospital or medical office where my health records experience will promote the accuracy, privacy, and convenience of patient records

SUMMARY OF SKILLS

Medical records management: ICD-9 coding and color-coded filing systems; proven commitment to customer service and patient privacy
Certification: CPHIMS and RHIT
Computer programs: AS400 and QuickBooks
Financial management: A/R, A/P, audits, contracts, orders, and vouchers

EXPERIENCE

Dr. Jean Rafael
106 Government Way, Coeur D'Alene, ID 83814
Office Manager, June 2002 to present
- Maintain records for all patients, including active and inactive files
- Compile reports for insurance records; reduced report generation time by 30%
- Handle accounts payable, accounts receivable, and payroll
- Use spreadsheet, database, word processing, and Internet software programs

Community Medical Center
1102 Sweetheart Lane, Coeur D'Alene, ID 83816
Intern, January 2001 to May 2002
- Greeted and registered patients
- Answered the telephones and scheduled appointments
- Assisted the bookkeeper with patient accounts

EDUCATION

College of Applied Careers, Spokane, WA
Associate of Applied Science, 2002
Major: Healthcare Information Technology; **Minor:** Accounting
Related Courses: Medical Terminology, Health Information Management, Clinical Classification, Health Law and Ethics, Financial Accounting, Cost Accounting
Certification: CPHIMS and RHIT

Figure 3.6 Model Personalized Resume (shown at 75% actual size)

Building a Resume with Wizards

Some career sites will not allow you to simply copy and paste your electronic plain-text resume into one field. Instead, you must "build" your resume by copying and pasting different sections of your electronic plain-text resume into separate fields. Wizards guide you through the process.

The resume-builder process is obviously more time consuming. However, it may prove worth your effort, for two reasons.

- ❑ The appearance and layout of built resumes is much more recruiter-friendly than plain-text resumes. They are typically formatted in an easy-to-read format that mimics a personalized resume.

- ❑ Built resumes are naturally separated into searchable segments. This allows recruiters and employers to fine-tune their keyword searches.

The resume that Marisa built at Monster® (**www.monster.com**) is shown in progress in **Figure 3.7** and completed in **Figure 3.8**.

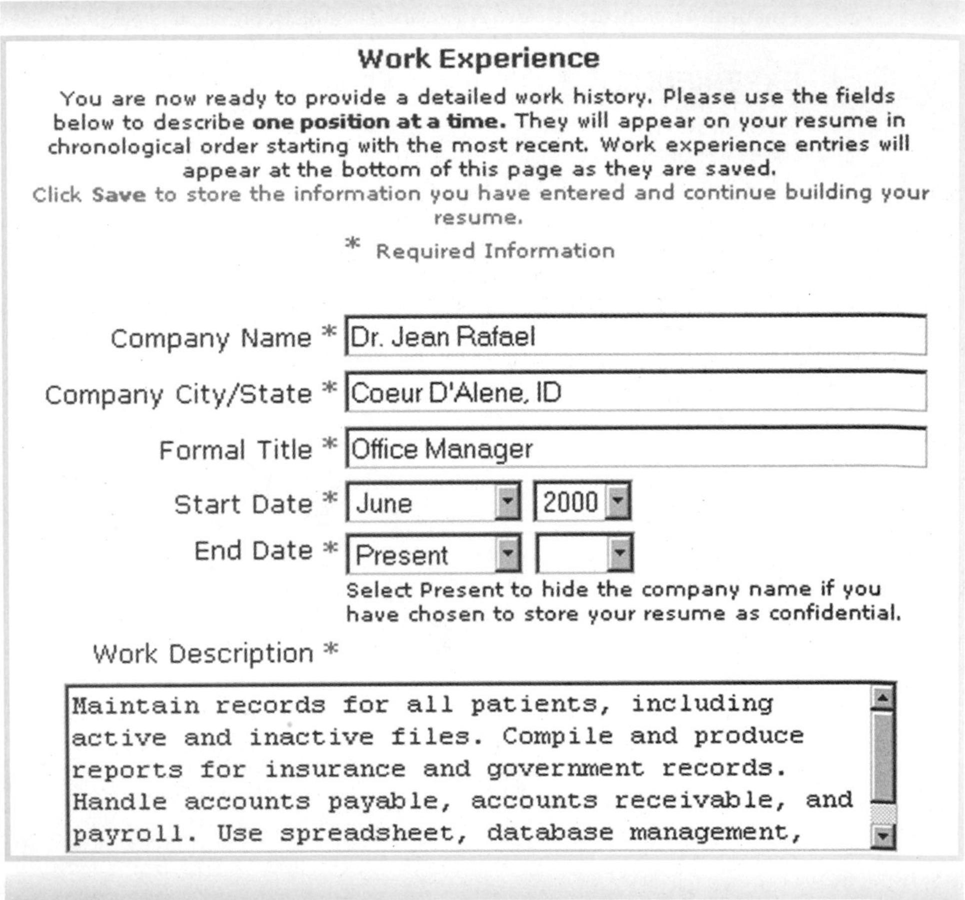

Figure 3.7 Model Built Resume, In Progress

© 2002 Monster. Reprinted by permission.

 monster

Marisa Georges
203 Apple Tree Lane
Coeur D'Alene, ID 83814
US
mrgeorges@live.net

Primary Phone:(208) 555-9087
Fax:(208) 555-6452

Medical Records Technician

Resume #21960329

OBJECTIVE	A position as a medical records technician in a hospital or large medical office

TARGET JOB

Desired Job Type:	Employee
Desired Status:	Full-Time
Site Location:	On-Site
Career Level:	Entry Level (less than 2 years of experience)
Date of Availability:	Immediately

TARGET COMPANY	**Category:**	Healthcare, Practitioner and Technician

TARGET LOCATIONS	**Relocate:**	No
	US-ID	

EXPERIENCE

6/2000 - Present   Dr. Jean Rafael   Coeur D'Alene, ID
Office Manager
Maintain records for all patients, including active and inactive files. Compile and produce reports for insurance and government records. Handle accounts payable, accounts receivable, and payroll. Use spreadsheet, database management, word processing, and Internet software programs.

1/2000 - 5/2000   Community Medical CenterCoeur D'Alene, ID
Intern
Greeted and registered patients. Assisted the bookkeeper with patient accounts.

EDUCATION

5/2000   College of Applied CareersUS-WA-Spokane
Associate Degree
Major in Healthcare Information Technology. Minor in Accounting.

ADDITIONAL INFORMATION

Medical records management: ICD-9 coding, color-coded filing systems. Certification: CPHIMS and RHIT. Computer programs: AS400 and QuickBooks. Financial management: A/R, A/P, audits, contracts, orders, and vouchers.

Figure 3.8 Model Built Resume, Completed
© 2002 Monster. Reprinted by permission.

Web Resumes and Portfolios

Though you don't *need* a Web resume and Web portfolio for your Internet job search, it certainly can't hurt to have them. Web resumes show recruiters and employers that you have technical savvy. Web portfolios are a useful way for job seekers to exhibit creative work that is not easily portable or that is best viewed in three dimensions. Examples include animated graphics, performance art, architectural models, and short films.

The Web site that hosts your resume and/or portfolio should not contain any personal elements, political affiliations, and personal photographs. (You should *never* provide a picture of yourself unless personal appearance is an integral part of your career, such as in acting or modeling.) Be sure your resume and portfolio Web site has no affiliation to your personal Web site.

Tips from the Pros

by Peter Newfield
President, Career Resumes (www.career-resumes.com)

The Five Most Important Things About Writing a Resume

1. A resume is written to impress, not to inform. Think of it as a marketing tool, not a historical record. Try to keep it to two pages—three if you are a senior executive.

2. The first page of your resume is valuable real estate—use it for your most impressive information. If you don't list any accomplishments in your resume, chances are no one will call you.

3. Visual presentation is as important, if not more important, than content. No one is going to take the time to read a traditional resume that is poorly presented.

4. No one cares if you are single or married, play the trombone, or enjoy league bowling. Personal information does not belong on a resume. *Never* include age, race, gender, religious affiliation (unless you are a member of the clergy), or blue ribbons for gardening.

5. Do not include the reasons you left or are leaving your job. *Never* mention "sexual harassment," "lawsuit," "workers compensation claim," or "fired me for no good reason." Some situations are better explained in person, if at all. Any phrases like the ones above will guarantee your phone will not ring.

Peter Newfield is president of Career Resumes and a managing partner of Your Missing Link (www.yourmissinglink.com). He is the "resume expert" for several leading job sites. He is also a career panelist for the Tribune Papers nationwide and the *Times Herald Record* in New York.

Formatting Your Web Resume

Web resumes come in two basic forms: electronic plain-text and electronic personalized. Though Web resumes are typically personalized, some job seekers post electronic plain-text resumes to their Web sites to give potential employers a one-stop shop—plain-text resume, personalized resume, and portfolio samples all in one place.

You can put more graphic elements in your Web resume than in your personalized resume. You can use every formatting element found in personalized resumes, plus conservative colors and graphics.

To format your Web resume using word-processing software, follow these steps.

1. Open your personalized resume, and select and copy the text.

2. Open a new document, and paste the copied text.

3. Save the new document as an **HTML** document with a name that designates it as your Web resume. HTML stands for hypertext markup language, which is the language used for creating Web sites.

4. Adjust your formatting elements.

5. Preview your Web resume in a Web browser. If you're happy with the formatting, publish it to your Web site. If not, reformat your Web resume, resave it as an HTML document, and preview it again.

To format your Web resume using Web page creation software, such as Microsoft FrontPage, follow these steps.

1. Open your Web page creation software or HTML editor.

2. Open your personalized resume, and select and copy the text.

3. Paste the copied text into your Web page creation software or HTML editor, or use the import feature.

4. Adjust your formatting elements.

5. If you're happy with the formatting, publish your resume to your Web site.

Marisa's Web resume is shown in **Figure 3.9.**

Checkpoint

1. Name at least three ways in which paper scannable resumes differ from electronic plain-text resumes.

_____

_____

_____

_____

2. When will you use an electronic personalized resume?

_____

_____

_____

_____

MARISA R. GEORGES

Address: 203 Apple Tree Lane
             Coeur D'Alene, Idaho 83814
Phone: (208) 555-9087
Fax: (208) 555-6452
E-mail: mrgeorges@live.net

OBJECTIVE

A position as a medical records technician in a hospital or large medical office

SUMMARY OF SKILLS

Medical records management: ICD-9 coding, alpha and color-coded filing systems
Certification: CPHIMS and RHIT
Computer programs: AS400 and QuickBooks
Financial management: A/R, A/P, audits, contracts, orders, and vouchers

EXPERIENCE

Dr. Jean Rafael
106 Government Way, Coeur D'Alene, ID 83814
Office Manager, June 20-- to present

- Maintain records for all patients, including active and inactive files
- Compile and produce reports for insurance and government records

EDUCATION

College of Applied Careers, Spokane, WA
Associate of Applied Science, 20--
Major: Healthcare Information Technology
Minor: Accounting

Figure 3.9 Model Web Resume

Creating Your Cover Letters

The Internet has drastically changed the way job seekers write and send **cover letters**. These letters are used to introduce a resume, and they are sent when submitting a formal application for a job opening. In an Internet job search, a traditional cover letter could be the last thing a potential employer will read. In fact, unless you are invited to an interview, your traditional cover letter is not likely to be read at all.

Employers simply don't have time to read thousands of lengthy cover letters. That translates to good news for you because you'll spend much less time writing cover letters. The cover letters you'll use most are much more efficient and much shorter! Nevertheless, they must be clear, concise, accurate, and well-written.

Short Cover Letter Basics

In addition to being much shorter, these new cover letters are always sent as e-mail text, generally as an accompaniment to an attached (or pasted) electronic plain-text resume. Your short cover letter e-mail should also be in "text only" or plain-text format with no special fonts, colors, or styles. A short cover letter should identify the specifics of the job opening and briefly state how you meet the employer's needs. Be sure to include the position title in the subject line of the e-mail.

When writing a short cover letter e-mail, or *any* business-related e-mail, be concise, avoid slang words, and check your spelling! In any cover letter, misspelled words, typing mistakes, and formatting errors are flaws that can cause your application to be rejected.

Short Cover Letter Components
The best formula for writing a short cover letter uses one short opening paragraph and a one-sentence closing statement.

- ❐ *Opening paragraph:* Briefly state the name of the position, the job number, and where and when you found the listing. Include a concise statement about how your skills and experience match the required qualifications.

- ❐ *Closing sentence:* Express interest in an interview or an opportunity to discuss the position.

When to Use Short Cover Letters
Depending on employer and recruiter requests and the level of the position you're seeking, you will use short cover letters for a large percentage of your responses to Internet job listings. Use a plain-text short cover letter when:

- ❐ You are responding to an online job advertisement.

- ❐ You are responding to a position advertised on a company Web page.

Activity 3.3: Short Cover Letters

Write a short cover letter for one of the job openings you found in Chapter 2. Use Marisa's short cover letter as a guide.

Model Short Cover Letter

To:	rdeangelo@alliedmedicalpartners.com
Subject:	Medical Records Technician Position (#Q62)

Dear Dr. DeAngelo:

I have attached my resume in response to the Medical Records Technician opening at Allied Medical Partners (#Q62), listed on www.monster.com on November 16. I hope you'll find my comprehensive medical office experience to be an excellent match for your needs.

I look forward to meeting you soon to discuss this opportunity.

Sincerely,

Marisa R. Georges
208-555-9087
mrgeorges@live.net

Your Short Cover Letter

Traditional Cover Letter Basics

A traditional cover letter is a sales device that describes why you are the person who should be hired for the position. It must convince the reader to invite you for an interview. Traditional cover letters should:

❐ Demonstrate knowledge about the organization and position you're applying for.

❐ Show how you meet the employer's needs.

Traditional Cover Letter Components

The best formula for writing a traditional cover letter uses three main paragraphs. Each paragraph has a particular function.

- ❑ **_Paragraph 1 (The Opening):_** Briefly state the name of the position and where and when you found the listing. Include a concise statement about how your skills match the required qualifications. Then focus on what you know about the company's accomplishments.

- ❑ **_Paragraph 2 (The Sales Pitch):_** Specifically describe how your experience uniquely qualifies you for the position. You may want to list your relevant experiences in a bulleted form for the second paragraph. Be careful not to simply reiterate the experience section of your resume.

- ❑ **_Paragraph 3 (The Closing):_** Begin your closing with a statement confirming that you are the person for the job. Then, express interest in an interview, and indicate that you will follow up with a phone call.

Because most traditional cover letters you send will be in a plain-text, e-mail format, they should not extend beyond the length of a computer screen. So keep your paragraphs brief!

When to Use Traditional Cover Letters

Though you'll rarely use traditional cover letters during your Internet job search, some situations will call for them. Like short cover letters, traditional cover letters will be sent as plain-text format e-mail messages. The only exception is when an employer specifically asks for a personalized resume and cover letter. In this case, you'll want to send a paper traditional cover letter that is formatted like your personalized resume and printed on matching 8½ × 11" paper.

Use a plain-text traditional cover letter when:

- ❑ You are responding to a high-level opening, such as an upper-management or major executive position.

- ❑ You are responding to a request to send a resume after a personal meeting or phone conversation with a recruiter or an employer.

Marisa's plain-text and personalized traditional cover letters are shown in **Figure 3.10** and **Figure 3.11**. Note that proper business letter format is shown in the personalized traditional cover letter.

◢ Checkpoint

Explain how short cover letters differ from traditional cover letters.

_____

_____

_____

_____

To: | rdeangelo@alliedmedicalpartners.com

Subject: | Medical Records Technician Position

Dear Dr. DeAngelo:

I was intrigued to find your opening for a medical records technician in the online classifieds of the Spokesman-Review on October 22. My experience and education in healthcare information technology and office management are an excellent match for managing Allied Medical Partners' records. Working for Allied Medical Partners would be a privilege, as I have followed your success at fighting for patients' rights with insurance companies over the past five years.

In December of 2002, I graduated from the Healthcare Information Technology program at the College of Applied Careers in Spokane, WA, with coursework in medical terminology and ICD-9 coding. I volunteered at the Spokane Free Clinic as an office assistant and worked as an intern at the Community Medical Center in Coeur D'Alene. I was hired immediately after graduation as an office manager for Dr. Jean Rafael, where I have honed my skills in medical records technology and office management. Recently, I successfully designed a new cross-referenced filing system for Dr. Rafael's office.

My belief in patients' rights and your success at negotiating with insurance companies are a nice match. I look forward to discussing how my skills can serve Allied Medical Partners' needs. I will call next week to inquire about a convenient time for an appointment.

Sincerely,

Marisa R. Georges
203 Apple Tree Lane
Coeur D'Alene, Idaho 83814
208-555-9087
Fax: 208-555-6452
E-mail: mrgeorges@live.net

Figure 3.10 Model Plain-Text Traditional Cover Letter (e-mail format)

Marisa R. Georges
203 Apple Tree Lane
Coeur D'Alene, Idaho 83814
(208) 555-9087
Fax: (208) 555-6452
E-mail: mrgeorges@live.net

(personalized inside address)

October 23, 2003   *(date at left margin)*

(4 line spaces)

Dr. Rhonda DeAngelo   *(letter address at left margin)*
Senior Partner
Allied Medical Partners
4306 Lanton Boulevard
Spokane, WA 99203

(2 line spaces)

Dear Dr. DeAngelo: *(salutation at left margin)*

(2 line spaces; body of letter starts at left margin)

I was intrigued to find your opening for a medical records technician in the online classifieds of the *Spokesman-Review* on October 22. My experience and education in health information technology and office management are an excellent match for managing Allied Medical Partners' records. Working for Allied Medical Partners would be a privilege, as I have followed your success at fighting for patients' rights with insurance companies over the past five years.

(2 line spaces)

In December of 2002, I graduated from the Healthcare Information Technology program at the College of Applied Careers in Spokane, WA, with coursework in medical terminology and ICD-9 coding. I volunteered at the Spokane Free Clinic as an office assistant and worked as an intern at the Community Medical Center in Coeur D'Alene. I was hired immediately after graduation as an office manager for Dr. Jean Rafael, where I have honed my skills in medical records technology and office management. Recently, I successfully designed a new cross-referenced filing system for Dr. Rafael's office.

(2 line spaces)

My belief in patients' rights and your success at negotiating with insurance companies are a nice match. I look forward to discussing how my skills can serve Allied Medical Partners' needs. I will call next week to inquire about a convenient time for an appointment.

(2 line spaces)

Sincerely,   *(complimentary close at left margin)*

Marisa R. Georges   *(4 line spaces with signature within)*

Marisa R. Georges   *(name of sender at left margin)*

Figure 3.11 Model Personalized Traditional Cover Letter (Business Letter Format—shown at 75% actual size)

It's a Wrap

❏ Though the traditional paper resume still plays a role, it will not be your only—or your most important—resume during your Internet job search.

❏ Computer-friendly resumes have less *style*—or formatting—so that computers can read them and more *substance*—or career-related keywords—so database searches can match skills to opportunities.

❏ Your Internet-ready resume will have three main formats: plain-text, scannable, and personalized.

❏ When a computer reads your resume, it's looking for career-related keywords.

❏ Your resume should identify your talents that apply to the career you're seeking and be simple, well-worded, and brief.

❏ Employers simply don't have time to read thousands of lengthy cover letters. The cover letters you'll use for your Internet job search are much more efficient and much shorter.

Learn the Lingo

Match each term to its definition.

Terms

___ **1.** ASCII	___ **10.** keyword search
___ **2.** Boolean search	___ **11.** paper resume
___ **3.** built resume	___ **12.** personalized resume
___ **4.** chronological resume	___ **13.** resume
___ **5.** cover letter	___ **14.** scannable resume
___ **6.** electronic resume	___ **15.** Web portfolio
___ **7.** functional resume	___ **16.** Web resume
___ **8.** HTML	___ **17.** wizard
___ **9.** keyword	

Definitions

a. a resume posted to a personal Web site

b. a special word related to a specific job and skill that is used to search computer databases

c. a resume that arranges work experience according to time sequence (most recent first)

d. an electronic collection of work samples, posted to a personal Web site, that can demonstrate skills and talents

e. American Standard Code for Information Interchange; a simple form of text that most computers can read and process

f. a letter that introduces a resume; sent when submitting a formal application for a job opening

g. abbreviation of hypertext markup language, the language used for creating Web sites

h. a resume that you build by inputting sections of your electronic plain-text resume into a wizard

i. a search for a specified word or phrase

j. a resume that is formatted to be read easily by a computer scanner

k. a resume that focuses on skills, personal attributes, and any relevant volunteer or job experience

l. a resume that is formatted with word processing software; your traditional formatted paper resume

m. a search that includes logical operators, such as *AND, OR,* and *NOT*

n. a document that summarizes your education, work experience, and skills

o. a computer guide that helps users through a series of steps to accomplish a task

p. a resume that is delivered in paper form

q. a resume that is delivered electronically

E-valuation

1. Using a job-board wizard, create a built resume. Copy and paste content from your electronic plain-text resume as needed. Do not activate your built resume (i.e., do not allow employers to view it)—you're only creating it for yourself at this point. When you've finished, answer the questions below.

   a. Did the wizard ask for content other than what was in your electronic plain-text resume? If so, what was the content? Are there sections you might consider adding to your base resume?

   b. Did the wizard offer any information about privacy or security? If so, what was the information? How do you feel about revealing personal data (your phone number, address, etc.) in your built resume?

2. If you originally created a chronological resume, rearrange the content to create a functional resume. If you originally created a functional resume, rearrange it into a chronological resume. What information, if any, did you need to add or delete to create your new base resume? Which style (chronological or functional) best demonstrates your skills and experience to employers? Why?

CHAPTER 4

CHAPTER OBJECTIVES

- ❏ Master the basics of Web searching.
- ❏ Learn to search for jobs within general and specific job boards.
- ❏ Learn to search for jobs within company Web sites.
- ❏ Learn to search for jobs in the online classifieds.

SEARCHING FOR YOUR TARGET CAREERS

Wildcards, spiders, and Booleans, oh my! Like Dorothy's quest to find the wizard in the film classic *The Wizard of Oz*, your Internet job search will involve many new obstacles and adventures. The Internet presents a variety of paths to your target careers—paths that are often plagued with wrong turns, worthless Web sites, and meaningless search results.

In order to navigate these paths successfully, you'll need a few good friends—tips and strategies that will help you avoid pitfalls and sharpen your search for a fulfilling career. In addition to offering general Web searching strategies and tips, this chapter will provide useful approaches to finding jobs within Web sites, locating company sites and company profiles, and using keywords effectively.

Model Job Seeker

Our model job seeker for this chapter is Allison. Allison is looking for work as a physical therapist. She'd like to live in Atlanta, Georgia, or Dallas, Texas, and would prefer a career that allows her to help people from all walks of life. Allison's experiences with searching for her target careers are provided as examples throughout this chapter.

Web Search Basics: Tips and Strategies

Imagine you've been paid to visit an international conference that will have 30 million people in attendance. While there, your mission is to get the names and e-mail addresses of people who own their own businesses, eat red meat, have more than three children, and live in the northeastern United States. Sound impossible? It would be! In fact, it would take several lifetimes to survey each person, one at a time, to find that specific information.

Today, there are approximately 30 million Web sites on the Internet. Without a firm grasp of how Web searches work, finding Web sites that host your target careers would be like searching for a needle in a haystack. Fortunately, there are many searching tools and methods that can help you find exactly what you're looking for in little time.

Understanding Web Searching Tools

A Web searching tool is a handy device that looks through a large database of Web pages to find information that matches a **query**—a question submitted to a search engine in the form of keywords. Web searching tools work very much like resume-tracking software. Instead of resumes, however, they search vast databases of Web pages.

Many people use the term *search engine* loosely. There are actually two types of Web searching tools, and they gather their database information in completely different ways.

- ❑ **Search engines** are databases of Web pages that are created by computer programs. These programs use a **"spider"** (or crawler) to scan the text in the Web pages for pertinent information.

- ❑ **Directories** are databases with Web site content descriptions that are developed by Web site owners or independent *human* reviewers. Directories don't cover as much ground as search engines, but they do favor Web sites that have accurate, useful content.

Many earlier Web searching tools utilized either spider-based search engines or human-reviewed directories. Today, a majority of Web searching tools will return results from both types of databases. However, these combination searches typically favor either search engine databases or directory databases when returning results. For example, Google™ (**www.google.com**) is a combination Web searching tool that focuses on search engine results, while Lycos® (**www.lycos.com**) is a combination Web searching tool that focuses on directory results.

How Search Engines Work

Knowing how search engines work will help you understand your query results. Search engines have three main parts.

- ❏ The spider (also called a crawler)
- ❏ The database (also called an index or catalog)
- ❏ The searching software

The search engine process works like this.

1. The spider reads all the text in a Web page, including titles and hyperlinks. It also follows links to other Web pages, reads all the text there, and so on.

2. The database or index receives all the Web site information the spider finds. This doesn't always happen right away—there is sometimes a small gap between the time when a Web site is "spidered" and when that information is put into the database.

3. A person enters a search query. For example, our model job seeker, Allison, is looking for online physical therapy periodicals, so she types the keywords *online physical therapy journal* into a **search field** (a text area where queries are entered, which typically looks like an empty box). See **Figure 4.1**.

4. The searching software scans the database to find the Web sites that contain the keywords in Allison's query. Any spidered information that is not yet in the database will not be searched.

5. The searching software ranks Web pages according to certain criteria, such as number and frequency of keywords found. The results are then returned to the user in order of rank.

How Search Engines Rank Web Page Results

Web searching software can scan millions of Web pages in seconds to find the results that are most relevant to a query. But search engines aren't human. We can't tell them what we're thinking, and they can't read our minds. So, how do they rank Web pages?

NOW YOU KNOW

The average Internet user does not look beyond the first 8 to 10 Web page listings from a Web search query. Disregarding results with lower rankings can be a big mistake! Though you'll often find a portion of what you're looking for in the first results, sometimes the 17th result—not the 1st—contains all the information you're looking for. Listings typically include a title and a brief description, so it won't take much time to peruse more results!

To rank the relevance of results, search engines use sets of rules, or mathematical equations, that filter Web pages based on the factors below. Though most search engines use the same factors to rank Web pages, they don't all use them in the same way. For example, one search engine might emphasize the importance of keyword location, while another might emphasize hyperlinks. That's one of the reasons that different search engines will give you different Web page results.

- ❏ **_Keyword location:_** The placement of keywords lets the search engine know how important those topics are in a given Web site. When filtering a Web site for keyword location, search engines look for keywords in the title (displayed in the window's title bar) and in the first few paragraphs of the main page or home page.

- ❏ **_Keyword frequency:_** In addition, search engines rank Web pages based on how often keywords appear in relation to other words.

- ❏ **_Hyperlinks (or links):_** Web sites are judged based on their number of hyperlinks and the relevance of these hyperlinks. (For example, do they also include keywords from the query?)

- ❏ **_Hits:_** Search engines will also rank Web sites based on the number of "hits" or mouse-clicks they receive when submitted in a results list. If a search engine's top-ranked Web page for *online physical therapy journal* never receives a hit, that Web page will not be listed first for very long. Likewise, a Web page that is ranked 15 by other criteria will climb the results list if it receives a lot of hits.

- ❏ **_Links from other pages:_** Search engines are now beginning to rank Web sites based on the number of other Web sites that provide links to them. If a large number of sites provide a link to a particular site, chances are that site is useful, accurate, and reliable.

Figure 4.1 Search Engine Search Field

Using Multiple Web Searching Tools

Unfortunately, no search engine database holds the complete contents of the Web. And every search engine uses slightly different equations for ranking Web site results. That's why you'll need to use more than one Web searching tool if you want to maximize your Web page results.

There are multitudes of Web searching tools that can help you find just about anything related to your job search. The following search engines, directories, and combination searching tools are among the best.

5 STAR WEB SITES

For more information about search engines and a directory of thousands of specialty search engines, visit
www.searchengineguide.com

❏ AllTheWeb®: **www.alltheweb.com**

❏ AltaVista®: **www.altavista.com**

❏ AOL® Search: **http://search.aol.com**

❏ Teoma℠: **www.teoma.com**

❏ Excite℠: **www.excite.com**

❏ Google™: **www.google.com**

❏ HotBot®: **www.hotbot.com**

❏ LookSmart℠: **www.looksmart.com**

❏ Lycos®: **www.lycos.com**

❏ Yahoo!®: **www.yahoo.com**

Improving Your Keyword Searches

Though Web searching tools do a pretty good job of searching and ranking Web sites, they don't always return your desired results. It is often said that a computer is only as smart as its programmer, and that output is equal to input. In other words, refining your input—the keywords you submit to search engines and directories—will improve your output—Web page results you can *use*!

Choose Your Keywords Carefully

Most problems with Web search results involve number and quality—receiving too many results, too few results, or irrelevant results. When submitting a keyword query to a search engine or directory, think of words that uniquely identify what you're looking for. The more distinctive the keyword, the more useful it will be.

When you receive no results or too few results:

❏ ***Be less specific.*** For example, instead of searching for *in vitro cardiac electrophysiology jobs*, try *cardiac healthcare jobs*.

❏ ***Use variations and synonyms.*** For example, a search on *biology **lab** jobs* or *biology **research** jobs* might produce more results than *biology **laboratory** jobs*.

❐ **Check your spelling.** Though some Web searching tools will catch and alert you to a keyword spelling error, they won't catch everything.

When you receive too many results or irrelevant results:

❐ **Be more specific.** For example, instead of searching for *education*, try *elementary school teachers* or *elementary school jobs.*

❐ **Use as many relevant keywords as possible.** For example, if you arc looking for organizations in your career field, try *medical transcription professional organizations* instead of *medical transcription.*

Searching with Operators

Whenever you enter more than one keyword into a search field, you are using a **search string**. A search string is a query consisting of more than one keyword that can be modified with searching features. Most Web searching tools will allow you to modify your search strings to maximize your Web page results. It's important to note that the following keyword search-string tips work for *most* search engines and directories. Remember to read each search engine's description and search options before performing a search!

Using Searching Math Operators

If you are relatively new to modifying search strings, using searching math operators is a great way to start.

❐ **The plus sign (+)**
+online +physical therapy +journal
Though some search engines will match cvcry kcyword in your query, others might not. The plus sign ensures that all of the words in your search string will be included in your results.

❐ **The minus sign (–)**
physical therapy –research
The minus sign allows you to search for Web pages that include some keywords, but not others. For example, the search string above will return physical therapy Web pages that aren't research-oriented.

❐ **Quotation marks (" ")**
"online physical therapy journal"
Putting search strings within quotation marks ensures that you only receive Web page listings that have all of your keywords in that exact order. Though this may exclude useful listings, it is a great way to target your results.

Combining Searching Math Operators

To further maximize your Web page results, you can combine searching math operators in numerous ways. For example, Allison wants to find the names of major physical therapy clinics in Atlanta, Georgia. However, she would rather not work in a hospital environment in Atlanta. The search strings below show two different ways Allison could enter this query.

"physical therapy clinic" +Atlanta –hospital
"physical therapy" +clinic +Atlanta –hospital

Using Boolean Operators

With the exception of quotation marks, Boolean operators work like searching math operators. You can use whichever functions you prefer! Boolean operators (*OR*, *AND*, and *NOT*) should be uppercase letters.

❑ **OR**
biology lab jobs OR biology research jobs
The *OR* operator finds Web pages that contain either or both of the keywords or keyword phrases.

❑ **AND**
elementary school teachers AND elementary school jobs
The *AND* operator works like the searching math plus sign (+).

❑ **NOT**
physical therapy NOT research
The *NOT* operator works like the searching math minus sign (–).

Combining Boolean Operators

Boolean operators can also be combined for better Web page results. Nesting—putting smaller Boolean search strings within parentheses—allows you to build more complex queries. For example, Allison is looking for the names of major physical therapy clinics in Dallas, Texas. This time, she wants listings for clinics *or* hospitals. In the search string below, Allison has "nested" *clinic OR hospital* in parentheses.

physical therapy AND (clinic OR hospital) AND Dallas

Using Wildcards

Wildcards are useful when you are unsure about the spelling of your keywords or when you want to search for plurals or variations of words.

❑ ***The asterisk (*)***
physical therap*
The asterisk allows you to search for all words that include the letters you enter. For example, the search string above will return results for *physical therapy, physical therapist,* and *physical therapists.*

- **The question mark (?)**
  network administrat???
  Each question mark represents one missing letter. For example, the search string above will return results for *network administrators* and *network administration*, but not *network administrator*.

- **The exclamation point (!)**
  graphic art!!!
  The exclamation point represents either one missing letter or no letters. For example, the search string above will return results for *graphic art*, *graphic arts*, and *graphic artist*, but not *graphic artists*.

Performing Advanced Searches

Most major search engines and directories provide an advanced search feature that gives you more control over how results are returned. Advanced searches vary greatly according to the Web searching tool you're using. Some commonly used advanced search functions follow. Take advantage of these features when they're available!

- **Match Any:** The *Match Any* feature works just like the Boolean operator *OR*. Use this feature when you're trying to get results for similar keywords, such as *writing*, *publishing*, and *editorial*.

- **Match All:** *Match All* works like the Boolean operator *AND* and the searching math plus sign (+). Results will include all the keywords in your search string.

- **Exact Phrase:** The *Exact Phrase* feature works like the searching math quotation marks (" "). Use this feature when you want all your keywords to appear together in a string.

- **Stemming:** Like the wildcard asterisk, stemming allows you to search for variations of keywords based on word stems. For example, a search for *software train* will return Web pages that include *software training* and *software trainers*.

- **Search by Language:** Most advanced searches allow you to select Web pages that are written in a particular language, such as English, French, or German.

- **Number of Results:** Some search engines will allow you to control the number of results from the main search field, but most place this feature in the advanced search. It's important to understand that when more than 10 results are displayed per screen, they typically provide only the hyperlink title and URL. You may need more information to go on!

- **Date Range:** This feature allows you to search for Web pages that have been posted within a certain time frame. Though this a useful feature, it is not consistently reliable. Unfortunately, Web page date postings aren't always accurate.

STATS

Searches pertaining to employment (e.g., *jobs*) are among the 25 most popular Web queries.

–www.wordtracker.com

Activity 4.1: Performing a Customized Search

Gather your searching gear—it's time to perform a customized Web search. Your objective is to use search queries to find useful Web sites for professional organizations in your career field. For each query you enter, record the Web searching tool and search string, advanced search features (if used), the best Web site found (name and URL), and a brief description of the site. A sample from Allison has been given to guide you.

Model Professional Organization Search

Search Tool and Query	Web Site	Summary
Yahoo! (advanced search on exact phrase): *physical therapy organization*	Physical Therapist Online (http://physicaltherapist.com/links/organ.shtml)	Jobs and hundreds of links to specific physical therapy organizations
HotBot: *"physical therapy" +organization*	TCAMS (www.voyager.net/tcams/abstracts/orgswww.htm)	Link to American Physical Therapy Association

Your Professional Organization Search

Search Tool and Query	Web Site	Summary

Diversify Your Efforts

Like search engines, there is no single job, career, or company Web site that contains every available job in your career field. That's why every successful Internet job seeker must be willing to diversify his or her searching efforts. It is crucial to explore every path that may lead to your target careers—you never know where they might be hiding.

Get Organized!

A diversified job searching effort will require a high degree of organization. In addition to the basic organization requirements of a traditional job search—tracking job listings, job contact information, and resume responses—you'll need to track and record where you've traveled, how you got there, and what you've seen.

- ❑ **Search with a purpose.** If you've ever surfed the Web, you know how easy it is to get sidetracked. You may begin researching coastal climate patterns but wind up looking at beach vacation spots. Before you start each search, have a firm purpose, such as *Finding Atlanta physical therapy clinic names and Web sites*. Write your purpose on a note, and keep it close by while you search.

- ❑ **Bookmark useful Web pages.** All Internet browsers will allow you to **bookmark**, or save, your favorite Web page addresses (or URLs) in an electronic list (sometimes called *Favorites*) for easy access. When you find a useful Web page, stop and save it with a descriptive name. When you need that Web page again, simply open your bookmark list and click on the hyperlink.

- ❑ **Keep a job search log.** Use a notebook, word-processing document, or spreadsheet to track your Web search activity. You'll want to include where and when you found job listings, thorough descriptions of those listings, job contact information, and useful search strings.

 Checkpoint

1. Explain the difference between a directory and a search engine. Name one advantage for using each type of Web searching tool.

_____

_____

_____

2. Why must you use more than one Web searching tool?

_____

_____

Searching the Job Boards

"Find your dream job!" "The fast track to a better job!" You've probably heard similar hype from job board advertisers. Though not all Internet job seekers find what they're looking for on the job boards, if your career field is well represented, and your desired locations are in major cities or are flexible, that hype may be close to the truth.

Searching within the job boards may be the easiest part of your Internet job search. Job board creators do everything they can to make searching within their sites simple and painless. Why? Because they want you to find work there! Job boards thrive on connecting employers with potential candidates—it's their business, after all.

The Major Players

There are numerous job boards, which range from the very specific to the very general. And new ones are popping up all the time. The following job boards are among the best of the general sites.

NOW YOU KNOW

Common job board advanced search options include:

- Search by career-related keywords
- Search by career field
- Search by location
- Search by salary range
- Search by employment type (full-time, part-time, etc.)
- Search by company name

❒ America's Job Bank (**www.jobsearch.org**). This site combines listings from the U.S. Department of Labor and state employment agencies.

❒ CareerBuilder® (**www.careerbuilder.com**). When you perform a career search at CareerBuilder, you're actually searching multiple databases from major job sites.

❒ HotJobs® (**www.hotjobs.com**). Though relatively new to the job board market, HotJobs has openings from a variety of career fields.

❒ Monster® (**www.monster.com**). Perhaps the most popular job board, Monster has vast general job and resume databases. It also offers expert career advice.

Searching Within the Job Boards

Job boards hold large databases of job listings—Monster® boasts more than one million listings. Though these databases don't come close to the large numbers of Web pages stored by Web searching tools, you wouldn't want to comb through each listing one at a time. That's why job boards with lots of listings use search engines that work like Web searching tools.

Job board search engines are typically easier to use than Web searching tools. They offer many advanced search options that allow you to build complex queries. You'll rely much less on searching math, Boolean operators, and wildcards to find what you're looking for. However, because searches can be customized by many different criteria, you'll want to perform multiple advanced searches for each job board.

Location Search:

```
——— Select all ———
Alabama-Anniston
Alabama-Birmingham
Alabama-Mobile/Dothan
Alabama-Montgomery
```

Job Category Search:

```
——— Select all ———
Accounting/Auditing
Administrative and Support Services
Advertising/Marketing/Public Relations
Agriculture, Forestry, & Fishing
```

Keyword Search:

```
[                                    ]
```

Figure 4.2 Job Board Search Field
© 2002 Monster. Reprinted by permission.

Finding Specific Job Boards

There are thousands of smaller job boards that cater to specific careers, industries, and special groups. Remember your professional organization search? Finding job boards through online professional organizations is one of your best bets for finding your target careers. You can also find job boards that cater to nonprofit organizations, diverse groups, industries, and location.

To find them, you'll conduct a more comprehensive version of your search from Activity 4.1. For example, Allison will search for job boards specific to her career field, special groups, industries, and desired locations.

5 STAR WEB SITES

For an extensive list of links to job boards by industry, check out **www. quintcareers.com/indres.html**

Activity 4.2: Job Board Search

This activity consists of three exercises.

- **A.** Search for Specific Job Boards
- **B.** Search Within Specific Job Boards
- **C.** Search Within Major Job Boards

Exercise A: Search for Specific Job Boards

Using your Web searching tool strategies, find at least five specific job sites for your career field, industries, location, and/or special groups. On a separate piece of paper, organize the sites you've found into a table. An example from Allison's search is provided to guide you.

Model List of Specific Job Boards

Web Site Name	Web Site URL	Type of Listings
Physical Therapist Online	http://physicaltherapist.com/links/organ.shtml	Physical therapy jobs
Essence Jobs	www.essence.com/essence/jobs/index.shtml	Jobs for black American women
Health Care Jobs Online	www.hcjobsonline.com	Jobs in the healthcare industry
Yahoo! Careers, Atlanta jobs	http://careers.yahoo.com	Jobs in Atlanta, GA

Exercise B: Search Within Specific Job Boards

Using your results from Exercise A, find at least five listings that match your target careers. Bookmark or print the listings. Organize them into a table similar to Allison's example below.

Model Job Listing From Specific Job Boards

Job Board	Job Title/ Date Posted	Company Name and Location	Brief Job Summary
Essence Jobs	Physical therapist (4/12/20--)	Kindred Health (Atlanta, GA)	Nursing and rehab center; good benefits

Exercise C: Search Within Major Job Boards

Search within three major job boards for at least five job listings. Bookmark or print the listings. Organize them into a table similar to Allison's example below.

Model Job Listing From Major Job Boards

Job Board	Job Title/ Date Posted	Company Name and Location	Brief Job Summary
Monster	Physical therapist (4/15/20--)	Round Rock Clinic (Dallas, TX)	Aquatic therapy, comprehensive evaluations, treatment plans

Checkpoint

1. What criteria do job board search engines use to refine queries?

_____

_____

2. List the keywords, search strings, and search strategies that helped you find job listings.

_____

_____

Searching Company Web Sites

Though job boards carry the most job listings, most e-recruiting happens through company Web sites. Searching for job listings through individual company Web sites is typically more time consuming than searching through the job boards, but it's well worth the effort.

Company Web sites provide valuable information about a company's products and services, work environment, and history. They can be a one-stop-shop for finding a job *and* performing company research.

Finding Company Web Sites

There are many different ways to search for company Web sites. Your search will depend on what you're looking for and what you already know.

- ☐ *Searching by company name:* If you know the name of the company, type it into the search field of a search engine or directory. Its Web site should appear within the first few results and will often be your first result. Use wildcards or stemming if you're unsure about the spelling.

- ☐ *Searching by industry or career field:* Many career-specific and industry-specific Web sites contain information about individual companies. Sometimes they even provide links to company Web sites.

- ☐ *Searching by location:* City government sites and city chamber of commerce sites will often list the names of local employers. Online city yellow page listings are also a great resource for finding company names within a location. Of course, you can also perform a general Web search, such as *"physical therapy" +clinic +Atlanta.*

- ☐ *Searching by company size:* There are numerous Web pages that offer large lists of Fortune 500 companies, the best mid-sized companies, the best small companies, and growing companies.

Web sites are prime vehicles for advertising and generating revenue. That's why most companies try to establish a URL that represents the company name—they want potential clients to find the site! When looking for company Web sites, try this trick: In the URL field of your browser, type www.**companyname**.com. Seven times out of ten, you'll go directly to the company's Web site!

NOW
YOU
KNOW

Searching Within Company Web Sites

Unfortunately, not all companies post available jobs on their Web sites. But most do. Company Web sites post listings in various ways, and finding them can often be challenging.

1. **Look in the main page topic bar.** Job postings are often included in the main topic bar on a company Web site's home page. This bar is typically displayed horizontally at the top of the page or vertically on the left side of the page. Look for main menu topics such as *Jobs, Opportunities, Employment*, or *Careers*.

2. **Go deeper.** Job openings are often hidden deep within company Web sites. If you don't find a topic related to jobs in the main menu bar, try main topics such as *The Company, About Us, Departments*, or *Human Resources*. Keep clicking until you find those listings!

3. **Look for the site map.** Some Web sites offer a site map link that allows you to view all the topics covered on the site. If the company posts its available jobs online, you'll find a link to them here.

4. **Perform a Web site search.** Some Web sites provide a search engine that looks for keywords (try *jobs, careers, employment*, or *human resources*) within the site. The Web site search engine is sometimes prominent, but often is hidden. (Look for *Search* links at the bottom of the page.) Most Web site search engines are not very sophisticated, so use this strategy as a last resort only.

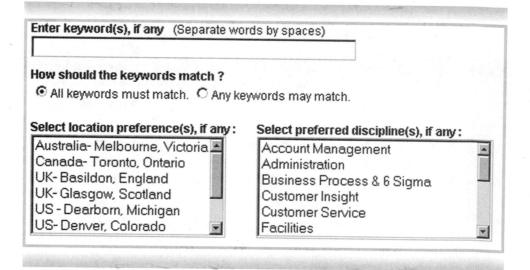

Figure 4.3 Company Web Site Job Listings
© 2002 Percepta, LLC. Reprinted by permission.

Activity 4.3: Company Web Site Search

This activity consists of two exercises.

A. Search for Company Web Sites
B. Search Within Company Web Sites

Exercise A: Search for Company Web Sites

Using your Web searching tool strategies, find at least 10 companies with job listings that fit your career target list. List one important thing about each company, and record where you found the job listings. On a separate piece of paper, organize the company Web sites you've found into a table. An example from Allison's search is provided to guide you.

Model List of Company Web Sites

Company Name and Location	Web Site URL	Job Listings Location	One Thing I Learned
Environmental Health Center (Dallas, TX)	www.ehcd.com/services/ physicaltherapy.html	Main topic bar (EHCD JOBS)	Founded by a pioneer in environmental and nutritional medicine
Easter Seals of Greater Dallas (Dallas, TX)	www.easterseals.com/ services	Main topic bar (Jobs and Volunteering)	Offers comprehensive services, including physical and occupational therapy
Beverly Enterprises (Atlanta, GA)	www.beverlycares.com	Main topic bar (Career Opportunities)	National chain of clinics offering many services

Exercise B: Search Within Company Web Sites

Using your results from Exercise A, find at least five listings that match your target careers. Bookmark or print the listings. Organize them into a table similar to Allison's example below.

Model Job Listing From a Company Web Site

Company Name and Location	Web Site URL	Job Title/ Date Posted	Brief Job Summary
Beverly Enterprises (Atlanta, GA)	www.beverlycares.com	Physical therapist (4/18/20--)	Performs evaluations, develops treatment plans to restore or compensate for loss of patient function

Checkpoint

1. List some advantages and disadvantages of looking for job listings on company sites.

_____

_____

_____

2. Describe a strategy for finding company sites or for searching for jobs within them.

_____

_____

_____

Searching the Online Classifieds

The Sunday newspaper employment classifieds have been a staple of traditional job searches for decades. Now, however, job seekers don't need to wrestle with piles of newspaper sections, inserts, and advertisements (unless they enjoy that sort of thing). Almost every major and minor newspaper in the United States has a companion news Web site.

To find classified listings from another city or state, yesterday's traditional job seekers had to use local library newspaper collections (which aren't always comprehensive) or subscribe to out-of-town newspapers (which usually arrive a few days after publication). Today's Internet job seekers can search up-to-date online employment classifieds for just about any location.

Finding Online Classifieds

Unless you're looking for work in a town with a population of 10, finding online newspaper classifieds should not be a challenge.

- ❐ If you know the name of the newspaper you're looking for, simply enter it into a Web searching tool search field.

- ❐ If you don't know the name of the newspaper you're looking for, try OnlineNewspapers.com (**www.onlinenewspapers.com**) for a comprehensive list of newspapers around the world that can be searched alphabetically or by region.

Tips from the Pros

by Todd Miller
Founder and CEO, SalesHeads[SM] **(www.salesheads.com)**

Sales and marketing people make the mistake of writing resumes as if they're accountants or programmers. List your accomplishments under your experience, in bullet points, on your resume...and focus on the dollars and cents. "Exceeded $5MM quota by 24%, in a mature territory, resulting in $2.5MM in gross profit" is an example.

Trying to get your *first* sales job? Read as much information as you can on modern selling techniques. Consider a sales training course that focuses on your chosen industry. A demonstrated willingness to learn will place you far ahead of the next person who doesn't have any experience.

Todd Miller is the founder and CEO of SalesHeads[SM], a leading Internet job board for sales and marketing professionals. He was also the founder and CEO of Selective Sales Staffing, an executive placement firm for sales and marketing professionals. Todd has been working with salespeople for more than 13 years, with experience ranging from entry-level through senior-executive sales management.

Searching Within Online Newspaper Classifieds

Online newspapers typically place classified employment links on the main topic bar of the Web site's home page. Most online classifieds provide a search engine that allows you to modify your search based on keywords, dates, and career fields. Online employment classifieds often provide additional job-seeking features, such as:

- ❑ Job banks that hold listings from local employers.
- ❑ E-mail notifications when a job appears that includes your career-related keywords.
- ❑ Career information and advice.
- ❑ Notification of career fairs.

Activity 4.4: Online Classifieds Search

Find at least five online classified advertisements that match your target careers. Bookmark or print the listings. On a separate piece of paper, organize the jobs you've found into a table. An example from Allison's search is provided to guide you.

Model Job Listing From Online Classifieds

Newspaper Name and Location	Web Site URL	Job Title/Company Name/Date Posted	Brief Job Summary
The Dallas Observer (Dallas, TX)	www.dallasobserver.com	Physical therapist, Casa Rehab Center (4/16/20--)	More than one position available; relaxed work atmosphere

Checkpoint

1. How have online newspapers improved job searches?

_____

_____

_____

2. In addition to classified job advertisements, what other career services do online newspapers provide? Mention any original features you found during your search.

_____

_____

_____

_____

It's a Wrap

❐ The Internet presents a variety of paths to your target careers—paths that are often plagued with wrong turns, worthless Web sites, and meaningless search results. In order to navigate these paths successfully, you'll need tips and strategies that will help you avoid pitfalls and sharpen your search for a fulfilling career.

❐ Today, there are approximately 30 million Web sites on the Internet. Without a firm grasp of how Web searches work, finding Web sites that host your target careers would be like searching for a needle in a haystack.

❐ Searching within the job boards may be the easiest part of your Internet job search. Job board creators do everything they can to make searching within their sites as simple and painless as possible.

❐ Though job boards carry the most job listings, most e-recruiting happens through company Web sites.

❐ Internet job seekers can search up-to-date online newspaper employment classifieds for just about any location.

> Never continue in a job you don't enjoy. If you're happy in what you're doing, you'll like yourself, you'll have inner peace. And if you have that, along with physical health, you will have had more success than you could possibly have imagined.
>
> –Johnny Carson
> Entertainer, former *Tonight Show* host

Learn the Lingo

Match each term to its definition.

Terms

___ **1.** bookmark
___ **2.** directory
___ **3.** query
___ **4.** search engine
___ **5.** search field
___ **6.** search string
___ **7.** spider

Definitions

a. also called a crawler, the part of a search engine that scans the text in Web pages for pertinent information

b. a query consisting of more than one keyword that can be modified with searching features

c. a database of Web pages that is created by computer programs

d. to save the address of a favorite Web page in an electronic list for easy access

e. a text area where queries are entered, which typically looks like an empty box

f. a question submitted to a search engine in the form of keywords

g. a database with Web site content descriptions that are developed by Web site owners or independent human reviewers

E-valuation

1. Choose a keyword or keywords related to your career target list (e.g., *veterinarian, healthcare, "physical therapist"*). First search for your keyword(s) with a combination Web searching tool that focuses on search engine results—try Google™ (**www.google. com**). Then search for your keyword(s) with a combination Web searching tool that focuses on directory results—try Lycos® (**www.lycos.com**). When you've finished, answer the questions below.

   a. Did the searching tools produce different results? List the URLs of the first two results from each searching tool.

   b. Which searching tool produced more useful and accurate results? Explain.

2. Which types of sites produced your best results: general job boards, specific job boards, company Web sites, or online classifieds? Choose the two types of sites that worked best for you, and find five new job listings for each type. Bookmark or print the listings. On a separate piece of paper, organize the jobs you've found into a table.

3. Assess the job listings you've found in this chapter. How well do they match your target career list from Chapter 2? Devise a brief job-hunting strategy for finding jobs that match your interests, industries, and career values.

> In order that people may be happy in their work, these three things are needed: They must be fit for it, they must not do too much of it, and they must have a sense of success in it.
>
> –John Ruskin (1819–1910)
> Victorian era artist and poet

CHAPTER OBJECTIVES

☐ Learn to evaluate the features and functions of job boards.

☐ Post your resume, profile, and personal settings on the job boards.

☐ Respond to job listings on the job boards.

JOB BOARDS

Imagine you're shopping for a new winter coat. Though you know the basic color and length you're looking for, you want to see a large variety of styles and fabrics. For this kind of shopping excursion, a large "superstore" specializing in coats would be your best bet.

Online job boards are like superstores for the Internet job seeker. Their job banks are crammed with job opportunities in a variety of career fields, locations, and salary ranges. To maximize your job board shopping experience, you'll need to know how to evaluate the merchandise, where to find the best selection, and whether you should pay a fee for extra services. In addition to offering valuable insider tools for understanding and evaluating job boards, this chapter will provide basic pointers for posting your resume, mastering profiles, using job search agents, and responding to job postings.

Model Job Seeker

Our model job seeker for this chapter is Ahmed. Ahmed is a passive job seeker with a bachelor's degree in management and six years of experience as a sales manager for a small financial services company. He would like to manage a sales team for a larger financial services company, and location is not important to him. Ahmed's experiences with posting his resume and responding to openings on the job boards are provided as examples throughout this chapter.

Evaluating the Job Boards

Your job search "safari" in Chapter 4 provided an assortment of job boards—from the very general to the very specific. As you wipe the dirt from your boots, think about which job boards worked best for you. Were they easy to navigate? Did they provide advanced search options? Did they offer lots of listings in your career field?

In addition to search capabilities and the number of job listings, there are several other factors to consider before posting your resume on a job board. It's important to understand that job boards don't necessarily protect your best interests. Some may allow third-party recruiters to circulate your resume without your consent, and others may charge fees for services that you probably don't need. When shopping the job boards to find work, remember the Latin saying *caveat emptor*—let the buyer beware!

Privacy and Confidentiality

Privacy—control over the public's access to your information—is a concern for *all* Internet job seekers. **Confidentiality**—control over a specific employer's access to your information—is a concern mainly for passive job seekers.

There are two main reasons to be concerned about privacy.

> **5 STAR WEB SITES**
>
> The Federal Trade Commission Web site offers comprehensive information about identity theft, including risk prevention, complaint procedures, laws, and current cases and scams. Visit **www.consumer.gov/idtheft/**

- *Identity thieves:* These unscrupulous folks frequently search for personal information in **open resume banks**, which are databases that are not protected with passwords. **Identity thieves** use your personal information to start credit accounts, to gain access to bank accounts, to obtain loans, and to commit other crimes that can seriously harm your finances and credit history. Unfortunately, most job boards have open resume banks.

- *"Reverse spamming" of resumes:* To **spam** is to send multiple copies of unsolicited mail or information to thousands of e-mail users. Spam is the equivalent of electronic junk mail. Reverse spamming involves taking someone else's information without asking, and sending that information electronically to thousands of people. If you place your resume in an open resume bank, it can be cross-posted to other open resume banks and/or third-party recruiters—without your consent or knowledge.

There is only one reason to be concerned about confidentiality—the boss! Passive job seekers must omit certain information from their online resumes (such as their names), and select certain confidentiality preferences during the job board registration process to ensure that their current employers don't find them out. Fortunately, there are ways to protect the privacy and confidentiality of your personal information.

To control who sees your Web resume (the resume you post to your own Web site), post it with an Internet Service Provider (ISP) that allows you to protect it with a password. When you give a potential employer your Web resume address (or URL), you can give them the password as well. This way, the only people who see or circulate your resume are the people you want to work for!

Activating Your Resume

Most job boards will require you to paste or build your resume during the registration process, and many will not allow you to search or apply for jobs *until* you have posted a resume. When your resume is stored on a job board, that doesn't mean you are obligated to share it with any potential employer. When posting resumes to job boards, you can:

- ❐ *Make your resume active.* This means your resume will be included in the searchable resume database. Any employer or third-party recruiter can view your resume when looking for candidates.

- ❐ *Make your resume inactive.* This means your resume will *not* be included in the searchable resume database. When you apply to a job listing on the job board, you'll either apply directly (by e-mailing your plain-text resume, for example) or through an automated *Apply* feature. Job boards that utilize automated *Apply* features automatically send your stored resume when you click the *Apply* button in response to a job posting. Inactive resumes are a great tool for passive job seekers. They can also be useful for active job seekers who want a higher level of privacy.

Privacy Tips for All Internet Job Seekers

Don't take identity thieves lightly. They can ruin your credit rating or mark your personal record with criminal activity. To keep your record clean:

- ❐ *Be careful about giving out your social security number.* Your social security number is the gateway to your personal record. Never put it on your resume! Likewise, unless a company is *very* well known, never submit your social security number when applying for a job.

- ❐ *Make sure your job board account is password protected.* Unfortunately, most job boards do not protect resumes with passwords. However, most *do* protect your personal account information with passwords.

- ❐ *Consider not activating your resume.* If you are truly concerned about privacy, don't activate your resume.

Confidentiality Tips for Passive Job Seekers

Supervisors often have internal human resources professionals search the Internet job boards to find current employees' resumes. To keep your boss in the dark about your job search, practice the following guidelines.

- ❐ *Utilize a job board that allows you to post your resume confidentially.* Some job boards, such as Monster® (**www.monster.com**), HotJobs® (**www.hotjobs.com**), and 6FigureJobs.com™ (**www.6figurejobs.com**), allow you to remove the contact information from your resume. Employers and/or the job board will then notify you via e-mail. Use an alias e-mail that does not give away your identity, such as *jss1@yourisp.com*.

❏ ***Consider removing the name of your current company from your resume.*** If you leave your company name on your resume, a competent human resources professional may figure out who you are.

❏ ***Do not provide your company e-mail address.*** Your company e-mail address can be a dead giveaway! For example, if your e-mail address is *jsmith@AmericanExpress.com*, you probably work for American Express. If you use your company e-mail in your resume *or* job board registration, job search agents and potential employers will send job leads to your work account. And remember, companies routinely track employee e-mail usage.

❏ ***Be careful about listing recognizable accomplishments.*** Be sure not to list any experience or accomplishments in your resume that can be tracked easily to your current company. Also, avoid the use of brand names or **proprietary** (exclusively company-owned) terms. For example, you wouldn't want to refer to your success with DeskJet printers if you worked for Hewlett-Packard or your input on the new Crest toothpaste if you worked for Procter & Gamble.

❏ ***Do not activate your resume.*** If you are extremely concerned about confidentiality, respond directly to company listings but don't activate your resume. Decide which is most important to you: not being "found out" or maximizing opportunities.

fact or myth?

If I block my company from accessing my job board resume, someone from my company might still find it.

It's a fact. Job board "company blocks" aren't foolproof. When companies register with the job boards, they enter their company names. When a company logs in to a job board to search a resume database, it is logged in as "Company A" or "Company B." When you choose to block a certain company from viewing your resume, the job board will only block employers who log in as recruiters from that company. If someone from your company logs in under a different name to search the resume database, he or she *can* find you.

The Downside of Confidentiality

Posting your resume confidentially is always a gamble. Though it's a great way to hide your intentions from your current employer, it can also hide your intentions (getting a better job) from potential employers.

- ❏ Recruiters in a particular industry often search for companies in similar industries. If your company name is omitted from your resume, you might miss good opportunities.

- ❏ Third-party recruiters and placement firms often post resumes confidentially. Many employers will assume that your confidential resume has been posted through a third-party recruiter and will likewise assume that they must pay a fee if they want to hire you. If employers think they have to pay a fee, they may be less likely to contact you for an interview.

- ❏ Human resources professionals will often import resumes from the job boards directly into their internal resume-tracking software. Companies that import resumes from job boards cannot use confidential resumes.

Should You Pay a Fee?

Though employers and recruiters must pay a fee to use the job boards, most job boards are free to job seekers. There are enough free job listings on the Internet that savvy job seekers should be able to avoid fee-based providers.

However, job boards are offering more and more fee-based services, such as bolded resume titles, automatic resume refresh, automatic registrations, resume writing, and resume "blasting." To learn more about these services, read the descriptions on each job board carefully. Then decide whether the services are worth the fee.

Though some of these services may be helpful, they certainly aren't necessary. An educated, organized job seeker like you can have a successful job search without utilizing any of them!

NOW YOU KNOW

Resume "blasting" is a fee-based service that sends your resume via fax or e-mail to thousands of companies and/or third-party recruiters. Some resume blasting services target your resume "blast" based on the target audience you're looking for, while others simply blast it out to the masses. The targeted resume blasting services provide the most value.

Understanding Cross-Posting

Many job boards share jobs by **cross-posting** listings. Cross-posting is the practice of sharing the same job listings on multiple job boards. It serves two main purposes.

- ❒ Cross-posting provides additional content for job seekers. If there are very few jobs listed, job seekers are not likely to return to the job board.

- ❒ Cross-posting creates a stronger selling proposition to employers and recruiters. For an additional fee, recruiters' job openings can be posted to other job boards.

Cross-posting is not necessarily a bad thing for job seekers. In fact, it can save you time and effort. However, you should try to be aware of whether a job board utilizes cross-posting, so that you don't waste time searching for jobs that you've already found! Web sites don't always reveal that they use cross-posting, but if they do, they'll usually put the information on the pages focused to job searchers or those focused to employers. Look for links or headings such as *Powered By* or *Job Distribution*.

5 STAR WEB SITES

Cross-posting sites combine job listings from many niche sites. They provide these postings to countless job boards. To get the job postings from the source, try these sites.
www.worklife.com
www.business.com
www.verticalnetmarketplaces.com
www.citysearch.com

The most common sites that utilize cross-posting are **portals**—Web sites that provide links and information to and from other sites. AltaVista® (**www.altavista.com**) and Excite℠ (**www.excite.com**) are good examples of portals. Using a "main source" for job listings is a great way to cover more ground.

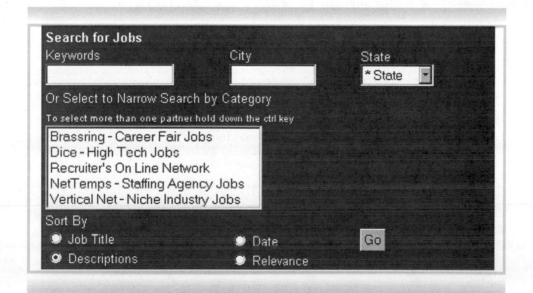

Figure 5.1 Portal Search Fields
© 2002 Entrepreneur.com, Inc. Reprinted by permission.

Activity 5.1: Job Board Evaluation

On a separate piece of paper, copy the job board evaluation criteria from Ahmed's example. Peruse at least 10 of your favorite job boards (from Chapter 4 and/or additional searches), and fill in a form for each one.

Model Job Board Evaluation Form

Job Board Name: Financial Jobs
Job Board URL: www.financial-jobs.com

1. **Number of jobs in your career field:** 117

2. **Number of companies listing jobs in your career field:** 83

3. **Name recognition: How did you hear about the site?** through a Web search

4. **Does the site feature employer sponsorships and/or cross-posting?** no employer sponsorships; cross-posting with other financial job boards (www.jobsinthemoney.com)

5. **Does the site list a phone number?** yes

6. **Are most of the jobs posted by direct employers or by third-party recruiters?** mostly direct employers

7. **When you call, does someone say the job board name?** yes

8. **How fresh are the jobs? Can you search by the date posted?** one week old, or older; no

9. **Does the site have a comprehensive privacy policy?** *(Read it!)* yes

10. **Do you have to register a profile or resume before you can search?** no

11. **Can you limit access to your personal contact information?** yes

12. **Will you be able to delete your resume after you've found a job?** not without calling

Checkpoint

1. Why must Internet job seekers be concerned with privacy?

   _____

   _____

   _____

2. List some disadvantages of posting a resume confidentially.

   _____

   _____

   _____

   _____

Putting Your Resume on the Job Boards

If you've never posted a resume on a job board, your first experience may be frustrating or exciting—or both! Depending on the site, it will take 10 to 20 minutes to post your resume and select your personal settings, such as privacy preferences.

You'll use the best job boards from your job board evaluation exercise to post your resume and respond to listings. Of course, you may add job boards at any point during your Internet job search. Just be sure to evaluate them before you use them.

Understanding Personality Profiles

Occasionally, job boards will have you fill out a **personality profile**—a "mini" self-assessment that gives potential employers a deeper look into who you are. Personality profiles are typically presented in the form of questions with multiple-choice answers and are built into the registration process (when you post your resume and submit your personal preferences). Personality profiles help employers pare down the pile of applicants by screening for suitability.

Though not all employers use personality profiles, you should try to identify the ones who do. Look for scoring on the job description (typically represented as numbers following a trait). If you are interested in the job, check your personality results with the target results to see if you are a match.

The online self-assessments listed in Chapter 2 provide good practice for personality profiles. You might want to take a few of the tests more than once to determine the relationship between your answers and the results.

Registration Matching

Some job boards use job seekers' registration information to generate matches. They capture job seeker information that is inputted through a series of entries during the registration process. They then run a query of the jobs that have been posted and:

1. Send employers a list of the job seekers that meet their criteria.

2. Send job seekers a list of the jobs for which they are qualified.

Though registration matching can be a helpful feature, don't rely on it solely. Because registration matching is performed automatically, you will not be able to adjust your search terms to get the best results.

Tips from the Pros

by Dwaine Maltais
Vice President of e-Recruiting Solutions,
Bernard Hodes Group (www.hodes.com)

Top Five Factors Employers Consider When Choosing a Job Board

1. Does the job board offer visibility and candidate traffic in relation to the specific job function? A site that either focuses on a select niche or offers niche content within a larger context often drives more focused traffic.

2. Is the job board localized? More and more employers are using localized job boards in addition to national or international boards, especially for entry-level or hourly jobs and jobs for which paying for relocation is not an option.

3. Does the job board direct interested candidates back to the company's corporate career Web site? This feature enables employers to utilize their own applicant-tracking systems instead of the job board's system or e-mailed responses. Applying directly through a company's Web site is often the fastest way to get noticed.

4. Is the job board easy to use? Posting and managing jobs should be a straightforward process.

5. Does the job board offer a searchable resume database? Many employers utilize online resume databases to actively search for potential candidates, and most job boards offer this as an add-on to the ability to post jobs.

Dwaine Maltais is the vice president for e-Recruiting Solutions of Bernard Hodes Group and leads the Hodes iQ program (www.hodesiq.com). He has developed industry-leading job-board evaluation and delivery technologies to help employers choose where to post jobs and capture job board metrics.
© 2002. Used with permission of the author.

Job Search Agents: Making the Job Boards Work for You

Job search agents are computer programs that search for jobs based on keywords that you choose. While you're busy with other facets of your Internet job search, these handy watchdogs periodically look for listings that match your keywords (e.g., *financial services* or *financial sales*). Job listing results are then returned to your e-mail account and/or your job board account.

To maximize the potential of job search agents:

❐ *Evaluate the quality of the results they provide.* Job search agents often retrieve scattered results, irrelevant jobs, and only a fraction of the relevant jobs. To test their effectiveness, start with one job search agent and a few targeted keywords, and analyze the results. You can do this by comparing the job search agent's results to the results of an actual job search query. Refine your keywords and try again until the agent provides better listings.

❑ ***Post multiple job search agents.*** Most job boards allow you to create three to five job search agents. Use them all to make sure that you cover all of the relevant keywords in your career field. If the site you are using only allows for one or two agents per user, create an additional user account (register again).

If you are an active job seeker, you should not rely solely on the results of job search agents. They can prove to be a valuable resource, but they by no means cover all of the positions on a job board. Each time you receive job results from a search agent, use them as a reminder to go back to the job board and perform another search on your own.

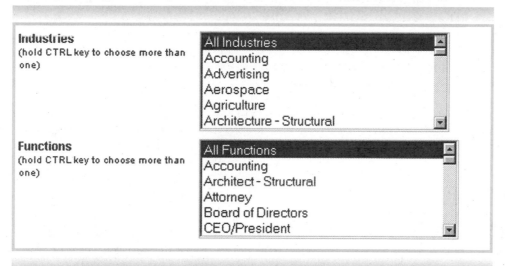

Figure 5.2 Job Board Registration Fields
© 2002 6FigureJobs.com. Reprinted by permission.

Job Board Registration

Unfortunately, there is no single way to register your resume, profile, and user preferences on all of the job boards. All job board registrations differ, and all offer different features and services. The following tips will help you master the registration process.

❑ ***Click through all of the options.*** Job boards try to make the registration process easy with step-by-step wizards and simple entry fields. However, you won't always find everything in one location. For example, account preferences, such as job search agents or privacy settings, may be under a different menu or link than resume posting.

❑ ***Troubleshoot keyword summaries.*** More and more job boards are using built resumes instead of pasted resumes. Though some resume builders will clearly mark where to paste your summary of skills (or keyword summary), you'll often have to determine where it goes by a process of elimination.

NOW YOU KNOW

Some job boards allow job seekers to "refresh" the time-stamp on their resumes with a click of a button. Take advantage of this option when provided. Resumes with outdated time stamps are often eliminated during a candidate search. You can also pay some job boards to automatically refresh your resume. Whether you do it yourself or pay the job board to do it, it's important to keep your resume date current!

STATS

There are roughly 30,000 job boards on the Internet, and more than 2 million online resumes.

☐ *Create resume "titles."* Most resume builders will ask you to give your resume a title. An effective resume title matches your desired job title (e.g., *Computer Programmer, Editor, Dental Hygienist*).

☐ *Watch for marketing surveys and advertisements.* Marketing surveys and advertisements are often enfolded in the registration process to make you believe that they are *part* of the registration process. Before you submit personal information, make sure the fields are required and check the headings on every screen.

Activity 5.2: Registering Your Resume, Profile, and Settings

Gather your list of job board evaluations—it's time to begin the registration process! For this activity, you'll want to have your electronic plain-text resume document open so that you can select, copy, and paste the text as needed.

Make sure to preview and check your registration information and resume before you activate your account. Print your resumes and profiles for your records, and record any specific information, such as registration usernames and passwords, in a table. A sample table from Ahmed is provided to guide you.

Sample Job Board Registration Table

Job Board	Username and Password	Date Posted	Job Search Agents/ Keywords Used	Other Options/ Comments
Financial Jobs	ahmedsinha sales2003	11/16/20--	None available	Anonymous resume posting; selected "sales" job category
HotJobs	asinha sales2003	11/16/20--	Created 3 search agents with same keywords	HotBlock privacy option

Checkpoint

1. Why should you use more than one job search agent?

_____

_____

_____

2. List some original job board registration tips. Draw from your experiences.

_____

_____

_____

Responding to the Ads

Your Internet job search is well underway! You've created your computer-friendly resumes, searched for listings, and posted your resumes. And your job search agents are busy hunting for matches. However, it's not yet time to sit back, relax, and wait for the job offers to come rolling in.

Even if you're in a high-demand career field and can move to any location, you'll still want to respond directly to job listings that fit your target careers. This way, you'll ensure that you find the jobs *you want*—not just the jobs that *want you*.

Getting Around the HR Gatekeeper

Company job listings are typically posted through the internal human resources (HR) department. However, the person who makes the decision to hire you is usually a department manager. HR professionals will narrow down large stacks of resumes before the person with the authority to hire even sees them. While you *don't want* to offend the HR department, you *do want* to increase your chances of getting noticed.

Sending your resume directly to the person who is hiring:

- ❑ Ensures that the person making the hiring decision sees your credentials.

- ❑ Gives you an opportunity to follow up with the decision maker.

- ❑ Provides an avenue for honest feedback. HR people are trained to be noncommittal in order to avoid controversy.

To get your resume in front of the person who has the authority to hire for the position:

1. Search the company's Web site to find out who the actual hiring authority is. The job listing will often state the title of the person you'll report to (e.g., *This position reports to the financial services manager*). Look for management bios. If you can't find the contact on the company Web site, call the company and request the name, title, and e-mail address of the person who is hiring for the position. Get the correct spelling!

2. Send your cover letter and resume directly to the person who is making the hiring decision. Though he or she might simply forward your resume to the HR recruiter, you might get a response. It's worth a shot.

NOW YOU KNOW

If you're a passive job seeker, make sure that you send your full resume—not your confidential job board resume—when applying directly to jobs.

ETHICS & ETIQUETTE

When calling a company for job contact information, be extremely polite and efficient. If companies wanted everyone to know the name of the hiring manager, they wouldn't filter resumes through the human resources department.

Identifying the Job Poster

In addition to postings from internal company recruiters, a large number of job listings on job boards are posted by third-party recruiters. Third-party recruiters stockpile scores of resumes so that they have a large pool to draw from when finding a match for employers. When the stack of resumes begins to shrink, some recruiters will resort to posting fake job listings. While most third-party recruiters post legitimate listings, be aware that some listings are merely bait for hooking resumes.

If you're not sure about which kind of listing you're dealing with, call or e-mail the contact person. Give the job description, and ask which company has the open position and which company that person represents. Though some third-party recruiters will protect the name of a legitimate hiring company until they've found a suitable match, you'll usually be able to tell if you're dealing with a real job or resume bait.

Some job boards, like HotJobs® and FlipDog.com™, allow you to filter your results to eliminate jobs posted by third-party recruiters and staffing agencies. If you don't see this option on a job board's search page, try clicking on *Advanced Search Page.* Not all job boards offer this option, though, so you may still have to call or e-mail the contact person to determine a job listing's source.

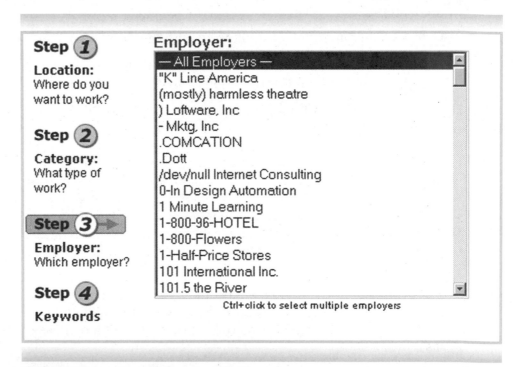

Figure 5.3 Internal Recruiter Contact Information
© 2002 FlipDog.com. Reprinted by permission.

Activity 5.3: Responding to Job Board Listings

To complete this activity, you'll need your job board listings from Chapter 4 (plus any new jobs you've found), and the resume documents you created in Chapter 3. Follow the steps below for each job listing.

1. Find out whether the job listing comes directly from the company or from a third-party recruiter. Call to ensure that the listing is legitimate.
2. Find the name of the person who is hiring for the position (through the company Web site or by calling the company).
3. Read the listing to determine which resume format and cover letter format to use. (Refer to Chapter 3 if you need a refresher.)
4. Send your resume and cover letter to the appropriate contact. Print and save e-mailed cover letters for your records.
5. Record the details of each response in a log or a table. A sample record from Ahmed follows.

Sample Job Board Response Record

Job Board/ Date of Application	Job Title/ Job Number/ Date Posted	Company/ Third-Party Recruiter	Contact Information	Type of Resume/ Cover Letter
Financial Jobs Applied 11/17/20--	Mutual fund sales manager Job 6911 Posted 11/08/20--	Zora Neale, Inc. Waltham, MA Direct company listing	Dina Page Title: CFO dpage@zora.com (781) 555-8600	Short e-mailed cover letter Electronic plain-text resume posted as e-mail text

Checkpoint

1. How can you determine if a job listing is legitimate?

_____
_____
_____
_____

2. Explain the advantages of "getting around the HR gatekeeper."

_____
_____
_____

It's a Wrap

❏ Online job boards are like superstores for the Internet job seeker. Their job banks are crammed with job opportunities in a variety of career fields, locations, and salary ranges.

❏ It's important to understand that job boards don't necessarily protect your best interests. When shopping the job boards to find work, remember the Latin saying *caveat emptor*—let the buyer beware!

❏ Depending on the site, it will take 10 to 20 minutes to post your resume and select your personal settings, such as privacy preferences.

❏ Even if you're in a high-demand career field and can move to any location, you'll still want to respond directly to job listings that fit your target careers. This way, you'll ensure that you find the jobs *you want*—not just the jobs that *want you.*

> Instead of thinking about where you are, think about where you want to be. It takes twenty years of hard work to become an overnight success.
>
> –Diana Rankin
> Author

Learn the Lingo

Match each term to its definition.

Terms

___ **1.** confidentiality
___ **2.** cross-posting
___ **3.** identity thieves
___ **4.** job search agents
___ **5.** open resume banks

___ **6.** personality profile
___ **7.** portal
___ **8.** privacy
___ **9.** proprietary
___ **10.** spam

Definitions

a. a job seeker profile created from self-assessment questions asked during the job board registration process

b. a Web site that provides links and information to and from other sites

c. computer programs that periodically search job board listings based on keywords that you provide

d. electronic junk mail; to send unsolicited mail or information to thousands of e-mail users

e. control over the public's access to your information

f. people who steal others' personal information to apply for credit or commit other crimes

g. resume banks or databases that are not protected with passwords

h. the practice of sharing the same job listings on multiple job boards

i. exclusively company owned

j. control over a specific employer's access to your information

> If you do not feel yourself growing in your work and your life broadening and deepening, if your task is not a perpetual tonic to you, you have not found your place.

–Orison Swett Marden (1850-1924)
Founder, *Success* magazine

E-valuation

1. Take out your job board response record, and calculate the following.

   a. The percentage of jobs that came from third-party recruiters vs. direct company listings

   b. The percentage of jobs that came from major job boards (such as CareerBuilder®) vs. smaller, niche job boards

   c. The percentage of jobs that called for electronic plain-text resumes vs. personalized paper resumes

   Do any of your findings surprise you? Why? How has your job board search compared to your original expectations?

2. Search the Internet for articles about confidential job searches. What strategies do companies use to monitor employee job searches? What measures do companies take when they find employees looking for new jobs?

3. Go to one of the job boards mentioned in this chapter and create a job search agent. When you receive a response from the agent, answer the following questions.

   a. Are the job listings provided by the agent useful and accurate? Explain.

   b. Using the criteria you provided to the job search agent, search for job listings on the same job board. Compare your results to the agent's results. Are they the same? With this knowledge, would you rely solely on an agent to perform your job search? Why or why not?

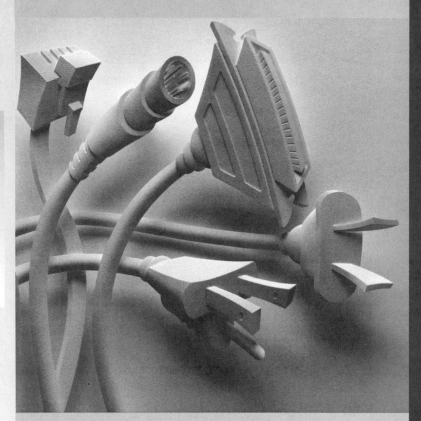
CHAPTER OBJECTIVES

❑ Expand your job search, discover strategies for getting inside companies, and apply for jobs directly through company Web sites.

❑ Understand the different types of search firms, and register your resume and profile with third-party recruiters.

CHAPTER 6

COMPANY WEB SITES AND THIRD-PARTY RECRUITERS

If you've ever been hungry at the grocery store, you've probably noticed that the power of a growling belly can override good judgment. When almost everything looks appetizing, a carefully planned grocery list falls to the wayside. Sometimes, an active job search can feel like shopping for food on an empty stomach. *Every* job opportunity starts to look appealing when you're hungry for work.

Though your Internet job search may provide many opportunities in your career field, it's important not to lose sight of your career target list. Going directly to company Web sites and third-party recruiters is one of the best ways to ensure that you find what you truly want. This chapter will focus on tips for performing in-depth company research, getting inside the right companies, and utilizing third-party recruiters.

Model Job Seeker

Our model job seeker for this chapter is Joyce. Joyce is a legal assistant for a small law firm in Rochester, New York, and has just finished her paralegal certification. Joyce's husband has been promoted to a position in a manufacturing plant in New York City, and the family is relocating in a few months. Joyce is looking for work as a paralegal in a family-friendly law firm with a flexible work schedule. In this chapter, Joyce will be applying for jobs through company Web sites and registering with search firms and recruiters.

Visiting Company Web Sites

If job boards are the superstores for Internet job seekers, company Web sites are the specialty shops. They offer job opportunities in your desired career field and industries, provide detailed information about company work environments, and contain jobs that aren't posted in other places.

Like specialty stores, however, company Web sites offer only a select number of listings at a given time, which translates to extra work for the Internet job seeker. In order to find the right fit, you'll want to visit several company Web sites and do some comparison shopping.

Your Company Search: Digging Deeper

As you discovered in Chapter 4, there are many different ways to search for company Web sites and company profiles. If company size, work environment, and/or location are important to you, you'll need to research possible companies carefully through chambers of commerce, phone directories, and other resources. This type of research can also be useful for learning more about companies you've found on the job boards.

5 STAR WEB SITES

For an amazing and useful collection of information about thousands of occupations, including projected employment needs and typical tasks, check out the U.S. Department of Labor's *Occupational Outlook Handbook* at **www.bls.gov/oco**.

Chamber of Commerce Directories
Chamber of commerce organizations often list major employers in a given city. For online directories of chamber of commerce Web sites for any city, state, or province, visit ClickCity.com (**http://clickcity.com**) or The Online Chambers (**http://online-chamber.com**).

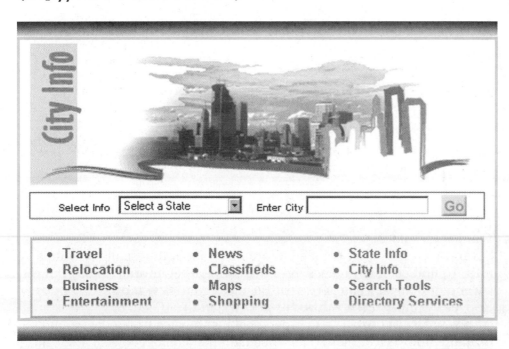

Figure 6.1 Chamber of Commerce Directory
© 2002 ClickCity.com, Inc. Reprinted by permission.

Telephone Directories

Online telephone directories are also a great resource for finding company names, addresses, and telephone numbers. To find companies by name or by category, visit AnyWho® (**www.anywho.com**). National compilations of yellow and white pages offering reverse phone number searches and searches for company types can be found at SMARTpages.com℠ (**www.smartpages.com**) and SuperPages.com℠ (**www.superpages.com**). For a repository of information from a number of sources, try InfoSpace® (**www.infospace.com**). To find the location of a phone number cited in a job board listing, try Switchboard® (**www.switchboard.com**).

Tips from the Pros

by David Bacharach
President, CS Information Technologies
(www.careersearch.net)

Top Five Company Research Tips

1. Recognize that many openings aren't advertised in newspapers or on job boards. But even when there aren't any openings, companies will often create them when they see attractive candidates who can offer them real value.

2. Because companies tend to hire from their competitors, try to focus on companies that offer similar products or services or that build on what you learned in your last position.

3. Try to explore how your skills or knowledge might be transferred to different types of jobs. For example, teachers might find positions in training or educational sales.

4. When searching company databases, be sure to use synonyms to cast a broader net. For example, if you are interested in the legal profession, try *counsel, attorney, law, lawyer, barrister,* or *legal.*

5. Try to avoid general, broad-based data sources. Search industry-specific content that is rich in contact names, titles, functions, and descriptive material. Specialists almost always have better, more comprehensive data in their field than do generalists.

David Bacharach is the founder, president, and CEO of CS Information Technologies, the creators of CareerSearch, of Needham, MA. He also frequently guest lectures to MBA students on entrepreneurial studies and using technology in the job search.

© 2002. Used with permission of the author.

Company Profiles

Several Web sites offer detailed information about thousands of companies. To find company names, profiles, and market information by industry and/or company category, visit Business.com (**www.business.com**), Hoover's Online℠ (**www.hoovers.com**), and WetFeet.com® (**www.wetfeet.com**). To find personal testimonies from current and former employees of more than 3,000 national employers, visit Vault Inc.'s research page (**www.vault.com/nr/researchhome.jsp**).

COMPANY RESEARCH

More than 3000 profiles of the world's top employers.

Enter Company Name   GO>

#abcdefghijklmnopqrstuvwxyz

[→] **Vault Reports and Career Guides**
The most powerful prep for your interviews, Vault's guidebooks are for sale as PDF downloads or shipped printed copies. You won't find information thi up-to-date, detailed, or "insider" anywhere else.

[→] **Vault Power Search**
Search for employers by location, industry, key stats and more.

[→] **Why Work for Us**
Our featured employers give their pitch on why YOU should become their next star.

Figure 6.2 Company Profile Web Site

Activity 6.1: In-Depth Company Search

Pull out the career target list you created in Chapter 2 and review the assessment of your ideal work environment. Using chamber of commerce, telephone directory, and company profile Web sites, find 10 to 30 companies that offer your ideal work environment. Record what you've found in a table. A sample from our model job seeker, Joyce, is provided to guide you.

Model Company Profiles

Company Name and URL	Contact Information	Profile
Law Office of Michael Weinstein www.mweinstein.com	1206 Park Ave., Suite 11 New York, NY 10016 (212) 555-4962 law@mweinstein.com	Divorce, family and criminal law, and bankruptcy 68 employees Large financial growth in early 2000s In-house daycare and flexible schedule
Wells & Dean www.wellsdean.com	302 Morningside Drive New York, NY 10023 (212) 555-3165 attorney@wellsdean.com	Employee representation: race, sex, age, religion, and pregnancy discrimination; severance agreements; medical leave Small, friendly work environment

OUACHITA TECHNICAL COLLEGE

Targeting a Company

Unfortunately, the companies you want to work for don't always advertise job openings geared toward your skills and interests. If you feel strongly about working for one particular company, resume seeding and employee referrals are two ways to get in the door.

Resume Seeding at Target Company Sites

If you want something to grow, you must plant a seed. **Resume seeding** means submitting your resume to target companies that have no current opportunities. It "plants" the idea of you as a potential employee and is an excellent way to get a leg up on your competition (who may not have shown such initiative). Even though you may not be hired immediately, you'll always be open to working in your ideal environment, right?

To increase the chances of landing your dream job, choose a target group of companies that you'd like to work for but that don't currently list job opportunities geared toward your interests and skills. Submit your resume to their Web site resume databases, or e-mail your resume to the main contact person. Be sure to include a short e-mailed cover letter specifying the type of work you're looking for.

Resume databases will typically hold your resume for three to six months. When a job *does* become available, you're already in the database! Remember to follow up and resubmit your resume every three months, and be sure to take advantage of job search agents when available.

Using Employee Referral Systems

You may have heard the business motto, "It's not what you know, it's whom you know." This motto also rings true for job searches: While *what* you know is certainly important, *whom* you know may be the key to finding an ideal job at your favorite company. **Employee referral systems** are programs that reward employees for referring candidates for open positions. These programs can encourage your contacts to help you in your search and make *whom* you know just as important as *what* you know.

Employee referrals tend to provide better fits with an organization, so HR departments often pay rewards to employees who refer candidates hired by the company. Open positions are usually available to current employees before they are posted on the Web. Therefore, you should ask everyone in your personal network of friends, family, and previous associates to look out for positions that match your skills and level of experience. Most of your contacts will do this happily, even if they won't be rewarded for the referral.

Activity 6.2: Responding to Company Web Site Ads

To complete this activity, you'll need your company Web site job listings from Chapter 4 (plus any new jobs you've found). Open the resume documents you created in Chapter 3, and follow the steps below.

1. Find the name of the person who is hiring for the position (through the company Web site or by calling the company).
2. Read the listing to determine which resume format and cover letter format to use. (Refer to Chapter 3 if you need a refresher.)
3. Send your resume and cover letter to the appropriate contact. Print and save e-mailed cover letters for your records.
4. Record the details of each response in a log or a table. A sample record from Joyce follows.

Model Company Web Site Response Record

Web Site/Date of Application	Job Title/ Date Posted	Contact Information	Type of Resume/ Cover Letter
Law Office of Michael Weinstein Applied 12/01/20--	Paralegal, divorce and family law Posted 11/25/20--	Chrystal Hill Divorce and family law attorney chill@mweinstein.com (212) 555-4962, ext. 23	Electronic plain-text resume posted in body of e-mail Short e-mailed cover letter

Checkpoint

1. Why should Internet job seekers perform thorough company research?

_____

_____

_____

2. Why do HR departments pay employees for candidate referrals?

_____

_____

_____

3. What percentage of your target companies have current job openings geared toward your interests and skills? Are your results similar to other students' results?

_____

_____

_____

Registering with Third-Party Recruiters

Third-party recruiters are like Web searching tools. They can't read your mind, but if you carefully tell them what you're looking for, they can be extremely helpful. Third-party recruiters should be genuinely interested in finding a good match for you. They receive payment if you accept a position, and successfully placing qualified candidates builds their reputation among job seekers and employers. Be cautious about a recruiter who seems to be more interested in quickly making as many matches as possible.

When registering your resume with a third-party recruiter, be sure to specify exactly what you want in a job. Talk about your career values, and give details that relate to your career target list, such as desired company size, work environment, location, salary, and benefits.

Contingency Search Firms

Contingency search firms are third-party recruiters who are paid only when they fill a position. In other words, their pay is **contingent** (dependent on something that may or may not occur) upon finding a match for the companies that hire them. Nearly all third-party recruiter job board listings come from contingency search firms.

Contingency search firms typically work with a large number of candidates and positions simultaneously. That's because their work is a numbers game—they have a much better chance of making matches when working with scores of jobs and resumes. Contingency search firms fill positions that range from entry level to senior management. Though they often have exclusive rights to a position, they typically compete with other search firms to fill the same positions. Thus, time is of the essence.

fact or myth?

I should register my resume with as many third-party recruiters as I can.

It's a myth. Internet job seekers often make the mistake of submitting resumes to too many search firms. As a result, their phone lines, e-mail accounts, and *lives* are overwhelmed with messages from third-party recruiters. Though you may think this is a good thing, it's important to realize that no job seeker has the time to organize messages that come in all day and night, every day of the week. And, unless you take the time to carefully explain your career needs to each third-party recruiter, most of the job leads you receive will not match your specifications.

Choose a few third-party recruiters who know what you're looking for and who demonstrate awareness of your needs by finding good matches. It may take some time to find the ones that work best for you, but it will be worth the effort.

When registering your job search with contingency search firms, choose a few national databases, as well as a few smaller firms in your desired locations and industries. Some of the larger national contingency search firms include:

- ❑ Kforce^{SM}: **www.kforce.com**

- ❑ MRI® (Management Recruiters International, Inc.): **www.brilliantpeople.com**

- ❑ Manpower® Professional: **www.manpowerprofessional.com**

Retained Executive Search Firms

Retained executive search firms are third-party recruiters who are paid in advance to fill executive-level positions. Employers **retain** (pay a fee in advance for) their services, regardless of whether they fill the position. Retained executive search firms are paid for their employees' skills, research, and contacts. They are hired on an exclusive basis and do not compete against other firms.

Retained executive search firm databases are usually one of the first sources recruiters use when performing searches for executive-level positions. These confidential databases typically require job seekers to register assessments or profiles before posting their resumes. Because there are usually very few positions, the average position has many qualified applicants and, therefore, takes more than three months to fill.

If you're looking for an executive-level position, you'll want to find retained executive search firms that commonly offer positions in your career field. The largest retained executive search firms include:

- ❑ e-Korn/Ferry^{SM}: **www.ekornferry.com**

- ❑ Futurestep™: **www.futurestep.com**

- ❑ Heidrick & Struggles International, Inc.: **www.heidrick.com**

- ❑ Spencer Stuart, Inc.: **www.spencerstuart.com**

- ❑ Russell Reynolds Associates, Inc.: **www.russreyn.com**

- ❑ Christian & Timbers: **www.ctnet.com**

The following three sites are great resources for information about search firms' locations and specialties. They also offer additional fee-based services that allow job seekers to search job databases, buy complete lists of executive search firms, and post their resumes to thousands of recruiters.

NOW YOU KNOW

Many search firm positions are confidential, and third-party recruiters may not be able to tell you who the hiring company is until the company agrees to meet with you.

If you are concerned about confidentiality, give recruiters the names of the companies you want to be shielded from. They will protect your privacy.

- Hunt-Scanlon Advisors: **www.hunt-scanlon.com**
- Kennedy Information: **www.kennedyinfo.com**
- Association of Executive Search Consultants: **www.aesc.org**

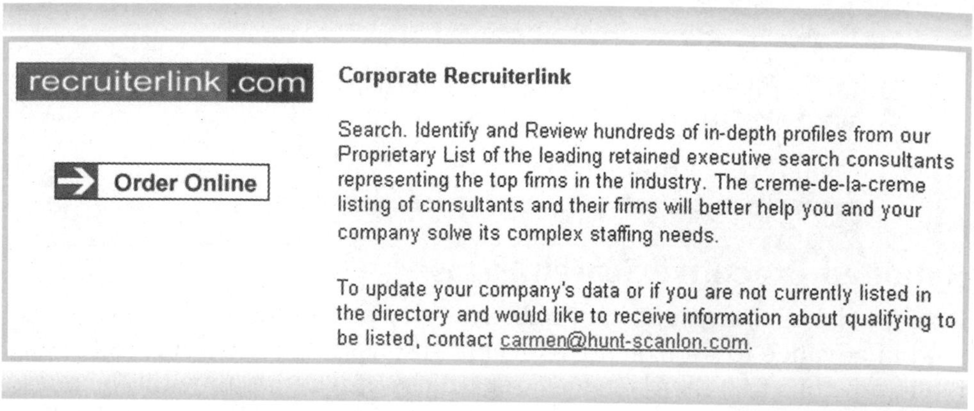

---

recruiterlink .com

→ Order Online

Corporate Recruiterlink

Search. Identify and Review hundreds of in-depth profiles from our Proprietary List of the leading retained executive search consultants representing the top firms in the industry. The creme-de-la-creme listing of consultants and their firms will better help you and your company solve its complex staffing needs.

To update your company's data or if you are not currently listed in the directory and would like to receive information about qualifying to be listed, contact carmen@hunt-scanlon.com.

Figure 6.3 Search Firm Information Site
© 2002 Hunt-Scanlon Corporation. Reprinted by permission.

Splits Systems

Splits systems are search firms that share job listings and candidate information and split any placement fees. To maximize your placement possibilities, try the following splits systems.

- Recruiters Online Network, Inc.: **www.recruitersonline.com**
- Top Echelon® Network, Inc.: **www.topechelon.com**

The Search Firm Hiring Process

After third-party recruiters research resumes, the process works like this.

1. The third-party recruiter will call you about an open position and ask questions to see if the position is a match.

2. If the recruiter believes you are a good candidate, he or she will send your resume to the company with the job opening.

3. If the company is interested, the recruiter will schedule an interview.

Activity 6.3: Registering with Third-Party Recruiters

Choose three to six third-party recruiters, research their standard job openings, and submit your resume to each firm. Be sure to contact the person who will be representing you and tell him or her about your specific job requirements. Make a record of your third-party recruiter contacts. An example from Joyce is provided to guide you.

Model Third-Party Recruiter Record

Search Firm Name and Type	Recruiter Contact Information	Types of Job Openings
The Counsel (www.thecounsel.com) Contingency search firm	Jerome Brown (212) 555-8104, ext. 773 jeromebrown@thecounsel.com	Legal jobs, including paralegal staffing in New York City

Tips from the Pros
by Scott Scanlon
Chairman and CEO, Hunt-Scanlon Advisors
(www.hunt-scanlon.com)

The most foolproof way to get on a headhunter's radar screen is to demonstrate your skillful career navigation. To be noticed by recruiters, you must show that you have managed your career wisely—you must be able to clearly demonstrate a consistent path leading toward your professional goals. Show recruiters that you have taken charge of your career and that you have handled various job transitions seamlessly. This clear track record will reveal that you are a focused professional and will set you apart from many individuals who have allowed their careers to take charge of them.

Smart headhunters and the world-class companies they represent always look beyond the bare essentials of your resume. Show them your personal aspirations along with your professional ones. Often, an intangible asset in your professional arsenal can make all the difference in the world—and put you head and shoulders above your competition. Show how you have performed as part of a team; highlight what you've done for your community. Above all, present yourself as well-rounded and well-grounded. That, along with your professional skills, should land you a face-to-face meeting with a headhunter—and a new start!

Scott A. Scanlon is chairman and CEO of Hunt-Scanlon Advisors, a market research firm tracking the headhunting industry. He has counseled hundreds of recruiters and thousands of individuals undergoing career transition during his 18-year career.
© 2002. Used with permission of the author.

Checkpoint

1. Explain how contingency search firms make money.

_____

_____

_____

2. Why might a third-party recruiter hide the name of a hiring company?

_____

_____

_____

It's a Wrap

❐ Though your Internet job search may provide many opportunities in your career field, it's important not to lose sight of your career target list. Going directly to company Web sites and third-party recruiters is one of the best ways to ensure that you find what you truly want.

❐ Company Web sites offer job opportunities in your desired career field and industries, provide detailed information about company work environments, and contain jobs that aren't posted in other places. But company Web sites offer only a select number of listings at a given time, which translates to extra work for the Internet job seeker.

❐ Third-party recruiters should be genuinely interested in finding a good match for you. Be cautious about a recruiter who seems to be more interested in quickly making as many matches as possible.

Learn the Lingo

Match each term to its definition.

Terms

___ **1.** contingency search firms
___ **2.** contingent
___ **3.** employee referral systems
___ **4.** resume seeding
___ **5.** retain
___ **6.** retained executive search firms
___ **7.** splits systems

Definitions

a. dependent on something that may or may not occur

b. programs that reward employees for referring candidates for open positions

c. submitting your resume to target companies that have no current opportunities

d. search firms that share job listings and candidate information and split any placement fees

e. pay a fee in advance for

f. third-party recruiters who are paid in advance to fill executive-level positions

g. third-party recruiters who are paid only when they fill a position

E-valuation

1. Choose four companies from the list you created in Activity 6.1. Search for information about each of the four companies at each of the four company profile Web sites mentioned in the chapter (**www.business.com**, **www.hoovers.com**, **www.wetfeet. com**, and **www.vault.com/nr/researchhome.jsp**). When you've finished, answer the following questions.

   a. Which site or sites provided the most comprehensive and informative results? Explain.

   b. Did you find information about all four companies at all four company profile sites? If not, which companies were missing from which sites?

   c. Based on the results of this search, which site or sites would you use for your future company information searches? Explain.

2. Perform an Internet search for news articles about the companies you researched in Activity 6.1. Try FindArticles.com (**www. findarticles.com**), or check the business archives of local online newspapers. Have there been recent layoffs or promising new product lines? Based on the information you find, re-evaluate your list of best companies, and order them from most to least promising.

3. Perform a similar Web search for news articles about the third-party recruiter search firms you researched in Activity 6.3. Try to find information about placement percentages and job seeker testimonies. Based on the information you find, re-evaluate your list of search firms, and order them from most to least promising.

" If opportunity doesn't knock, build a door. "

-Milton Berle
Comedian and actor

CHAPTER OBJECTIVES

❏ Discover strategies for conducting a long-distance job search, giving relocation information to potential employers, and finding online job listings in small towns.

❏ Apply to jobs in your target locations using online classifieds, geographic job boards, and government job sites.

LOOKING FOR LOCATION

CHAPTER 7

It has been said that there are no shortcuts to any place worth going. This may be true of just about everything except job hunting on the Internet. While the Internet won't literally transport you to new locations, it will provide many shortcuts for targeting specific locations. If you're relocating, the Internet will help you find almost anything you need for your move—including a job in your new town.

The Internet is truly a blessing for job seekers who prioritize location because it provides a means of virtually scouting out and visiting a location before you arrive. This chapter will provide strategies for conducting your Internet job search by location. Whether you're staying home, going home, or relocating to a new place, you'll discover proven ways to home in on your target locations.

Model Job Seeker

Our model job seeker for this chapter is Sin-Feng, a quality assurance manager in a manufacturing plant. Sin-Feng is a passive job seeker from Tallahassee, Florida. He is planning a move to Raleigh, North Carolina, to take advantage of the massive job opportunities in the Research Triangle Park area. Sin-Feng's experiences with searching for jobs in his target location are provided as examples throughout this chapter.

The Location-Specific Job Search

If location is one of your significant career values, you're in luck. When you want to live in only one or two target locations, an Internet job search can take on a real sense of purpose—and considerably less time. Internet job seekers value location for a variety of reasons. Some simply cannot move from their home towns, some want to move closer to loved ones, and some may just prefer a particular environment.

Of course, if your target locations have small populations or modest employment outlooks, your Internet job search may take a little longer than average. Your job hunting strategy will also vary quite a bit depending on whether you're off to explore new lands or planning to dig deeper roots in a familiar place. Whether you're staying or leaving, you'll enhance your list of target companies if you research regional job sites, visit local government sites, and delve further into online job classifieds.

Targeting Your Home Town

If you're staying right where you are or going back to a familiar place, the ability to network and make contacts offline can improve your job search. If you're staying in or moving to a town you know well:

- ☐ Take advantage of local business contacts, such as friends or relatives who work in your town.

- ☐ Make more local business contacts by seeking temporary employment or voluntary work.

- ☐ Utilize the career services of the local universities, employment agencies, job fairs, and newspapers.

Relocating

If you're relocating to an unfamiliar place, the purpose you'll gain from a location-specific job search can be exciting—you'll inevitably learn more about your new home-to-be as you search for jobs. A long-distance job search requires a little extra research, planning, and skillful timing, but it can be well worth the effort.

STATS

According to James E. Challenger of the *Chicago Sun Times,* in the first half of 2000, only 21% of job seekers relocated to take a new job. That is down 17% from an already low 25% of job seekers who relocated in the first six months of 1999.

Scoping It Out

Internet job seekers who are relocating have a distinct advantage over traditional job seekers who are relocating: They can *virtually* scope out the job scene before they arrive. To find out who's hiring, who's firing, who's growing, and who's starting up, you can search online newspapers and business publications for articles about local employment patterns and outlooks.

Giving Relocation Information

Though an employer will typically assume that you are willing to move (otherwise, you wouldn't be applying for the job), directly stating your relocation intentions shows employers you are a genuine prospect. If relocation is critical, consider stating your intention to move in your resume objective (e.g., *Relocating to Raleigh to use my skills in …*). Otherwise, state your relocation intentions in your short e-mailed cover letter or longer traditional cover letter.

If you're moving to a new town regardless of whether you've found employment, mention the time of your expected arrival in the first paragraph of your short or traditional cover letter (e.g., *I am relocating to Raleigh in late June.*). This solidifies your commitment to the move.

However, if you are letting job offers dictate where you go, think about who will be paying your moving expenses before you directly state your relocation intentions.

☐ Job seekers in high-demand or executive-level career fields can expect most potential employers to pay their moving expenses. If you are in demand or at the executive level, you might not want to mention your relocation directly, as doing so may imply that you are prepared to pay your expenses. It's best to leave it open and hope that the employer will offer to pay. Moving expenses can sometimes be the deciding factor between two comparable job offers.

☐ Most employers won't offer to pay moving expenses for job seekers who are neither executives nor in demand. And many will view your relocation as a slight disadvantage. Moving can delay starting dates, and some candidates decide not to make the move after the offer has been accepted and other candidates have been turned down. For these reasons, you might want to directly state in your cover letter that you are *willing* to pay moving expenses. This lets prospective employers know that you'll trek across the country to follow the job for little or no relocation assistance.

Finding Your Contacts

Nearly 70 percent of job seekers find jobs through networking. That's one of the reasons that a long-distance job search can be challenging: It's difficult to network in a new city if you don't know anyone! Try the following tips:

- ❑ Talk to your family, your former employers and coworkers, your friends, your teachers, your neighbors, members of professional organizations, and anyone else who may have a contact in your new location(s).

- ❑ Make contacts online through job-related bulletin boards. Be careful, however, about giving away personal information if you're a passive job seeker.

- ❑ If you have time, attend conferences, trade shows, and job fairs in your new location(s). Or, attend conferences in your current location and seek out attendees from your target location(s).

- ❑ Contact third-party recruiters in your new location(s). (Refer to Chapter 6 for a refresher on how to choose a search firm.)

- ❑ If you have identified specific companies you'd like to work for, check to see if they have offices or divisions near your target location(s).

City Lights or Green Pastures?

Large cities provide many online job possibilities and job research avenues. Many smaller towns, however, don't even have specific regional job sites. And, job board searches by location often turn up results in big cities. To find job opportunities in a small town, be prepared to look a little deeper. In addition to your job board and company Web site searches, you'll want to:

- ❑ Perform several Web searches using search strings that combine the name of your town and job-related information (e.g., *Smallville jobs, Smallville employment, Smallville employers, Smallville industry*). Don't forget to bookmark useful sites.

- ❑ Comb the online yellow pages for names of local companies. Then perform a Web search for those companies to find their Web sites.

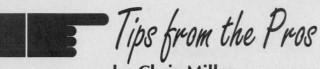

Tips from the Pros
by Chris Miller
Founder and Former CEO, 6FigureJobs.com™
(www.6figurejobs.com)

Strategies for Internet Job Seekers

Network. As a rule, you should make an effort to stay in touch with contacts throughout your career. But if you haven't done so to date, now is the time to call on your network of friends and acquaintances. Take advantage of alumni, professional associations, and local career transition support groups.

Search for jobs. Visit online job sites. Search for jobs by location and by areas of interest and industry. If there's a certain company you'd love to work for, you'll probably find a job section right on the corporate site. And don't forget traditional classified ads.

Apply. Send your resume and cover letter by the means specified in the ad. These days, it is typically suggested to e-mail or apply through a site.

Research the company. Familiarize yourself with the company's history, locations, vision, etc. Know about its industry and competitors. Sites like Hoover's Online℠ (**www.hoovers.com**), Vault Inc. (**www.vault.com**), and Redbooks™ (**www.redbooks.com**) are great resources.

Interview. You should spend two hours preparing for each interview. Know yourself like a product. Have examples ready that demonstrate your skills in leadership, problem solving, etc. Be early to the interview, and make sure to have several fresh copies of your resume. Steer the conversation from *getting* the job to *doing* the job. Ask questions. Many strong candidates bring a notepad with prepared questions and extra pages for notes. This simple act shows you are serious about the job and helps the interviewer recognize the professional, efficient manner in which you conduct yourself.

Follow up. It doesn't matter how you follow up after interviewing, just that you do. Handwritten letters are still impressive, but in this day of fast decision-making and high-speed technology, an e-mailed thank you will certainly suffice.

Chris Miller is the founder and former CEO of 6FigureJobs.com™. He has spoken at numerous conferences covering such topics as online recruiting, executive career development, professional networking, and career services.
© 2002. Used with permission of the author.

Checkpoint

1. List two reasons for providing an employer with relocation information.

_____

_____

2. Create a tip for finding contacts in a new town or finding online job listings in a small town.

_____

_____

The Location-Specific Job Sites

If you're like most job seekers, you have one to three target locations. And if those target locations don't include New York City, Chicago, Los Angeles, or another major metropolitan location, you may experience some difficulties finding listings on the job boards.

In the following exercises, you'll delve into three major resources for location-specific job listings. You'll dig deeper into online newspaper classifieds, mine **regional job boards** (job boards that provide job listings specific to a city, state, or region), and explore government sites. Even if you have a major metropolis in your list of target locations, though, your search will still benefit from the many location-specific resources available online.

Online Newspaper Classifieds

As you discovered in Chapter 4, online newspaper classifieds are a great resource for location-specific job openings. Online newspapers tend to be strong regional players, sometimes offering the most comprehensive coverage for certain areas. Most online newspapers also list openings in addition to those found in the classified ads, and large employers often post expensive **display advertisements** (large advertisements with graphic elements that are separated from print-only advertisements) on online newspapers to advertise important or multiple positions.

Keep in mind that newspapers usually charge by the line for printed advertisements, which means that most classified ads are short and to the point. Because online classified ads mirror printed classified ads, they are generally much shorter than traditional Internet job postings. To produce the best results, search by job title or position.

5 STAR WEB SITES

For more links to national classified job listings, visit the following sites.

www.careerjournal.com	**www.boston.com**
www.usatoday.com	**www.careerbuilder.com**
www.newspaperlinks.com	**www.newsdirectory.com**
www.nytimes.com	**www.newslink.org**

The Advantages

In addition to offering listings geared to a particular location, online newspaper classifieds provide many other advantages for job seekers with specific target locations.

- Online classifieds generally provide the strongest local and regional job coverage.

- Smaller companies tend to use regional newspapers for their job listings because they are generally cheaper than posting ads in one of the larger national job boards, such as Monster® or HotJobs®.

- Because online classifieds can be searched by specific criteria, they are much more efficient to use than printed classifieds.

The Disadvantages

While online newspaper classifieds will be one of your most reliable sources of location-specific job postings, they do have limitations.

- Online newspaper classifieds don't always include every listing from printed newspapers. Some, for example, don't post display ads.

- Smaller newspaper sites have limited job-seeking tools.

- Many online newspaper classifieds do not include a significant percentage of Internet-only job postings. That means you'll be competing against every job seeker who reads the newspaper.

- Unlike the job boards, online classifieds generally provide more fax numbers and URLs than direct e-mail addresses of recruiters and hiring managers. If you don't have a fax machine, try an online faxing service, such as FaxResume (**www.faxresume.com**).

Tips from the Pros

by Jason Krebs
Vice President of Sales and General Manager,
***The New York Times* on the Web (www.nytimes.com)**

It is important for job seekers to include newspaper sites like **www.nytimes.com** or **www.boston.com** in their job searches. These sites provide an integrated print and online strategy, so that all of the jobs posted in the newspaper can also be found online. Additionally, these sites provide access not just to local employment opportunities, but also to a national marketplace of companies that are seeking qualified candidates.

Most major newspaper sites, especially those for newspapers in larger cities, provide career-related articles, company information, e-mail alerts, and other tools designed to simplify the job search. In addition, job seekers can access the newspaper's archived business and finance articles for more information about a specific company or the city's economic climate.

Jason Krebs is the vice president of sales and general manager of *The New York Times* on the Web. He previously served as vice president and general manager of classifieds for *The New York Times* on the Web and Boston.com and before that as vice president and general manager of *The New York Times* on the Web's *New York Today* page.

Activity 7.1: Responding to Online Classified Ads

To complete this activity, perform an in-depth online search for classified ads in your target location(s). Don't forget to look at the national online classified listings. Combine what you've found with the online classified ad listings you found in Chapter 4. Open the resume documents you created in Chapter 3, and follow the steps below.

1. If possible, find the name of the person who is hiring for the position (through the company Web site or by calling the company).
2. Read the listing to determine which resume format and cover letter format to use. (Refer to Chapter 3 if you need a refresher.)
3. Send your resume and cover letter to the appropriate contact. Print and save e-mailed cover letters for your records.
4. Record the details of each response in a log or a table. A sample record from Sin-Feng follows.

Model Online Classified Ad Response Record

Web Site/Date of Application	Company/Job Title/Date Posted	Contact Information	Type of Resume/ Cover Letter
The News & Observer (www.newsobserver.com) Applied 06/15/20--	RTP Industries (Raleigh, NC) Quality Assurance Department Manager Posted 06/12/20--	Hudson Brown President hbrown@rtpind.com (919) 555-1687, ext. 21	Electronic personalized resume sent as e-mail attachment Traditional e-mailed cover letter

Regional Job Boards

Regional job boards were a relatively new phenomenon just a few years ago. Now they seem to be popping up everywhere. Though regional job boards are typically geared to larger cities, you will find sites that focus on states (e.g., jobs in North Carolina) or regions (e.g., jobs in the southeast United States).

The Advantages

If your target locations are specific to a state or region rather than to a city or town, state and regional job boards can save you a lot of time. And, if you're targeting large cities, you'll typically find more than one regional job board for each location. Using a simple Web search, Sin-Feng found more than 10 regional job boards for the greater Raleigh area.

To find regional job boards, enter a basic search query, such as *Raleigh jobs*, into a Web searching tool.

NOW YOU KNOW

The Disadvantages

Occasionally, a small town *will* host a useful regional site. However, like the major job boards, most regional job boards focus on large cities. Because many regional job boards are just becoming established, they don't all offer lots of listings. Often, regional job boards contain listings that are cross-posted in other locations. Be aware of the job posting dates, and understand that you may be applying for jobs that are listed on other sites.

Activity 7.2: Responding to Regional Job Board Ads

To complete this activity, perform a Web query to find regional job boards in your location(s). Combine what you've found with any regional job board listings you found in Chapter 4. Open the resume documents you created in Chapter 3, and follow the steps below.

1. If possible, find the name of the person who is hiring for the position (through the company Web site or by calling the company).
2. Read the listing to determine which resume format and cover letter format to use. (Refer to Chapter 3 if you need a refresher.)
3. Send your resume and cover letter to the appropriate contact. Print and save e-mailed cover letters for your records.
4. Record the details of each response in a log or a table. A sample record from Sin-Feng follows.

Model Regional Job Board Response Record

Web Site/Date of Application	Company/Job Title/Date Posted	Contact Information	Type of Resume/ Cover Letter
Raleigh Jobs (www.raleighjobs.com) Applied 06/16/20--	Eckert & Brink Diagnostics (Raleigh, NC) Production Plant Manager Posted 06/12/20--	Sami Wells CEO samiwells@eckertandbrink. com (919) 555-9971, ext. 76	Plain-text resume sent as e-mail text Traditional e-mailed cover letter

STATS

According to the Bureau of Labor Statistics, more than half of federal workers hold managerial or professional jobs, which is double the rate of the workforce as a whole. And about four out of five federal employees work outside of the Washington, D.C., metropolitan area.

Government Sites

Government sites typically post their listings by location, making them a great resource for job seekers who target specific areas. Government sites come in two varieties.

- ❒ *Government career sites:* Government career sites post available jobs in city, state, or federal government industries. Many large cities offer federal government jobs. If your target location is a large city and/or a state capital, try city, state, and federal sites. For smaller towns, check out the city government career sites. To find them, enter a Web search query such as *City of Raleigh employment* or *Raleigh government careers.*

- ❒ *Government employment agencies:* Most cities and states have **government employment agencies,** city and state organizations that provide general employment opportunities in a given area. These agencies are set up to maintain employment rates in their locations and typically work in conjunction with unemployment departments. Though a percentage of the listings come from newspaper classifieds and other job boards, many of the jobs are posted only on these sites. Beware: Some city and state employment agencies will require you to apply for the jobs through their services. To find government employment agencies, enter a Web search query such as *City of Raleigh employment agency, Raleigh unemployment,* or *North Carolina unemployment.*

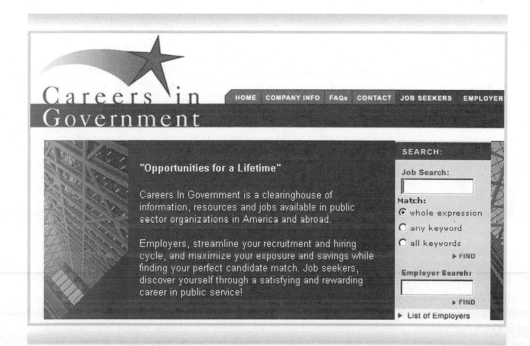

Figure 7.1 Government Career Site
© 2002 CareersInGovernment.com. Reprinted by permission.

Tips from the Pros

by Mark F. Weinberg
Chief Operating Officer, CareersInGovernment, Inc.
(www.careersingovernment.com)

Top Five Tips for Obtaining Government Employment

1. Take the time to learn about what differentiates public sector employment from private sector employment. There are many differences in terms of organizational structure and culture, compensation models, and management and labor rights and relationships.

2. Learn about the industry. Most people understand that Marriott operates hotels and General Motors manufactures automobiles. The levels and business of government operate in the background for most of us and can be more obscure and complex.

3. Assess both your suitability and desire to devote a career to public service. You will need to communicate your reasons clearly in your resume and oral interview.

4. Expect and prepare for a structured testing protocol as part of the selection process. Government hiring is characterized by objective, merit-based competition that often includes written, oral, and even practical examinations. Many testing aids and guides are commercially available.

5. Do your homework. Government has an "open architecture": Information about how it works and the community it serves is accessible to all. There is a greater expectation for you to come to your interview knowledgeable about the elected officials, the agency's fiscal condition, and the current local issues.

Mark F. Weinberg is co-creator and COO of CareersInGovernment, Inc., which works to match qualified individuals with careers in government and the public sector and allows more than 20 million Americans working, or seeking employment, in public sector occupations to exchange news and information. He is also the deputy city manager of Inglewood, CA (population 120,000). He has 30 years of local government public service experience.

© 2002. Used with permission of the author.

5 STAR WEB SITES

For links to government job listings, visit the following sites.

www.usajobs.opm.gov	**www.federaljobs.net**
www.careersingovernment.com	**www.statelocalgov.net**
www.govexec.com/jobs	**www.govtjobs.com**
www.govtjob.net	**www.fedguide.com**
www.jobsfed.com	**www.firstgov.gov**
www.statejobs.com	**www.fedworld.gov/jobs/jobsearch.html**

Activity 7.3: Responding to Government Site Ads

To complete this activity, perform a Web query for government job sites and government employment agencies in your location(s). Gather your job listings, open the resume documents you created in Chapter 3, and follow the steps below.

1. If possible, find the name of the person who is hiring for the position (through the company Web site or by calling the company).
2. Read the listing to determine which resume format and cover letter format to use. (Refer to Chapter 3 if you need a refresher.)
3. Send your resume and cover letter to the appropriate contact. Print and save e-mailed cover letters for your records.
4. Record the details of each response in a log or a table. A sample record from Sin-Feng follows.

Model Government Site Response Record

Web Site/Date of Application	Company/Job Title/Date Posted	Contact Information	Type of Resume/ Cover Letter
City of Raleigh (www.raleigh-nc.org/ mis/employ.htm) Applied 06/16/20--	City of Raleigh Wastewater Treatment Plant Manager Posted 06/10/20--	Helen Walters Personnel Manager hwalters@raleigh-nc.org (919) 555-6098, ext. 12	Plain-text resume sent as e-mail text Traditional e-mailed cover letter

Checkpoint

1. Why is a smaller company likely to use newspaper classifieds?

_____

_____

_____

2. What's the best way to find regional job boards? Give an example.

_____

_____

_____

3. Explain the two basic types of government sites. Which type provided the best listings for your career target list?

_____

_____

_____

It's a Wrap

☐ If you're relocating, the Internet will help you find almost anything you need for your move—including a job in your new town.

☐ Whether you're staying or leaving, you'll enhance your list of target companies if you research regional job sites, visit local government sites, and delve further into the online job classifieds.

☐ If you're like most job seekers, you have one to three target locations. And if those target locations don't include New York City, Chicago, Los Angeles, or another major metropolitan location, you may experience some difficulties finding listings on the job boards. Even if you have a major metropolis in your list of target locations, though, your search will still benefit from the many location-specific resources available online.

Learn the Lingo

Match each term to its definition.

Terms
___ **1.** display advertisements
___ **2.** government employment agencies
___ **3.** regional job boards

Definitions

a. job boards that provide job listings specific to a city, state, or region

b. large advertisements with graphic elements that are separated from print-only advertisements

c. city and state organizations that provide general employment opportunities in a given area

E-valuation

1. Perform a Web search to find employment trends and statistics in your target location(s). Look for employment percentages, industry breakdowns, and employment breakdowns by job titles or career fields.

2. Perform a Web search to find city sites geared toward people who are relocating. List 10 things you discovered about your new town or the town you're staying in. Include city services, arts and entertainment, industry, and neighborhoods in your list.

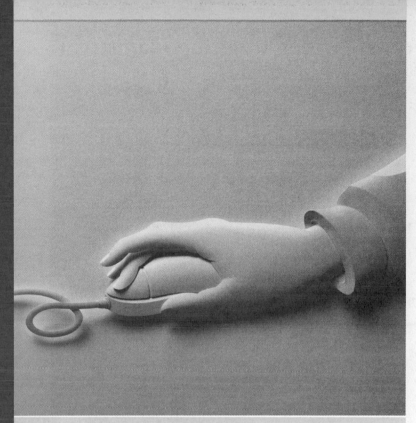

CHAPTER OBJECTIVES

☐ Discover the types of specialty sites, and understand the advantages and disadvantages of using them.

☐ Find and apply for job listings on a variety of specialty sites.

USING SPECIALTY SITES TO YOUR ADVANTAGE

CHAPTER 8

Despite the tens of thousands of jobs of every description that are listed on the major job boards, many terrific jobs still never make it there. If you have an unusual profession or if you want to work for a small company or nonprofit organization, you might not find the job of your dreams on one of the big job boards. Instead, you should focus your search on the thousands of smaller, specialized job sites, which focus on unique professions and work environments.

Even if your career skills and needs are considered mainstream, specialty sites can provide options that uniquely fit your career target list. In this chapter, you'll discover how to apply your Internet search skills to finding and applying to job listings on a variety of specialty sites—including nonprofit sites, diversity sites, and newsgroups.

Model Job Seeker

Our model job seeker for this chapter is Carmela, who has a bachelor's degree in psychology. Carmela plans to eventually earn a master's degree and counseling certification to become a psychiatric social worker. For now, she wants practical experience working with troubled children as a residential counselor. Carmela has worked part-time in the psychiatric unit of a major children's hospital for the past two years. She is bilingual in Spanish and English, which is a valuable work asset. Though Carmela would like to remain in her home state of Florida, location is not as important to her as other aspects of her work environment.

Specialty Sites: Out of the Mainstream

A number of Web sites have evolved to suit out-of-the-mainstream employers and job seekers. These **specialty sites**—Web sites that post job listings for specialized, or "niche," career fields or groups—have been developed to target certain segments of the job market. There are thousands of specialty sites, and they are as varied as the Internet itself.

Though some specialty sites are difficult to categorize, most fit into one of the five following groups.

- Professional and career association sites
- Industry and business association sites
- Diversity sites
- Nonprofit sites
- Newsgroups

fact or myth?

Working for a large employer will give me increased job security.

It's a myth. Large employers regularly downsize their workforce to enhance efficiency, sometimes by as much as 20 percent. And even large employers can undergo enormous business reversals, because of acquisitions and mergers or new management, in which up to 50 percent of employees can be laid off.

The best job security an employee can have is excellent work skills, people skills, and the ability to deal positively with change. It also pays to keep your job search skills up to date!

Why Employers Use Specialty Sites

Most employers post their job openings on one major job board (such as Monster® or HotJobs®), one regional site, and one specialty site. But some employers only post to specialty sites. There are a number of reasons why.

- Employers who don't hire often may not find the large job boards as convenient and as economical as they would if they hired more often.

- Employers whose workers have specific and unusual skills (e.g., an art conservation studio) may have difficulty finding trained, experienced technicians on a general job board.

- **Nonprofit organizations**—groups, agencies, or institutions whose goals do not include making money—do not usually pay wages comparable to those in the corporate world. Nonprofits often prefer to recruit candidates who understand nonprofit pay scales.

These employers are in the minority, but they've found that specialty sites allow them to get the word out to the specific kinds of job applicants they want. Instead of contracting with the large job boards, they post their job openings to more specialized sites that don't generate as much volume but yield a higher percentage of successful matches for their particular needs.

The Many Faces of Specialty Sites

Some specialty sites belong to large corporate recruiters and some, at the other extreme, are hosted on personal Web pages. Most, however, fall somewhere between the two extremes in terms of commerciality and number of hits.

- ❐ Some are structured primarily for job seekers, while others post jobs as just one of many site functions.

- ❐ Some maintain their own job boards, while others only provide links to selected job boards.

- ❐ Some allow you to post your resume, while others do not.

- ❐ Some require you to register or subscribe before you can search the job listings, while others allow you to search listings without registering or subscribing.

Professional and Career Association Sites

Most **professional associations** (organizations that promote, and sometimes set standards for, a profession), such as the North American Association for Environmental Education (**www.naaee.org**) or the Association for Women in Communications (**www.womcom.org**), maintain Web sites designed to fulfill the needs of individual association members. Employment opportunities are an important feature of many of these sites, which may provide their own job boards, links to other job boards, or both. Some professional association sites maintain so many links to job boards that they function effectively as career portals.

One potential disadvantage of professional association sites is that many, especially those that maintain their own job boards, do not permit access to non-members. This is a practical reason for job seekers to join professional associations relevant to their career fields.

Industry Association Sites

Like professional associations, **industry associations** (organizations of businesses, institutions, or other entities that promote, and sometimes set standards for, an industry) also maintain Web sites designed to fulfill the needs of association members. In this case, however, the members are

In 2000, women were paid 73 cents for every dollar men were paid in comparable jobs. At that rate, over a lifetime of work, the average 25-year-old woman could lose more than $523,000 to unequal pay.

–AFL-CIO

employers rather than job seekers. So, if an industry or business association maintains a job board, it is generally open to the public, not just to members.

Most industry association Web sites maintain their own job boards. This is especially true for associations of employers who need employees with unusual experience or skills. For example, the American Association of Museums (**www.aam-us.org**) operates its own job board and also provides links to member organizations with available jobs. Even if an industry association does not host its own job board, it will often maintain links to members' Web sites, which nearly always post job listings.

Diversity Sites

Diversity sites are designed to fulfill the needs of job seekers who belong to minority groups or other groups that commonly face discrimination, usually because of a difference in age, race, sex, religion, or physical or mental ability. Some diversity sites focus on job listings, while others offer a job board as only a small part of their overall mission. Diversity sites also tend to offer support materials or features, such as advice for mainstream success and links to helpful resources.

NOW YOU KNOW ⟹

National and international service programs, such as the Peace Corps (**www.peacecorp. gov**) and Ameri-Corps (**www. americorps.org**), provide volunteer and paid opportunities. Many private organizations offer similar opportunities, sometimes in the form of internships. Most of these organizations use the Internet to recruit workers.

Diversity sites usually list mainstream jobs at companies that are strongly committed to diversity and make a point of recruiting minorities. In addition, some may list jobs that require skills specific to a particular language or culture. For example, a Latino site may list jobs requiring native fluency in Spanish or familiarity with rural Guatemalan culture.

Some highly specialized diversity sites, such as the National Society of Black Engineers (**www.nsbe.org**), do not post jobs but instead maintain a board on which members can post resumes. These sites focus on the needs of their members and can be a valuable warehouse for information, support, and networking.

Nonprofit Sites

Unlike most companies, nonprofit organizations do not exist to make money. Their missions are typically philanthropic (e.g., to help people achieve better lives, to advance scientific knowledge, to free people who are wrongly imprisoned, or to conserve natural areas). People work in the nonprofit sector because they believe strongly in the missions of the organizations they work for. Many people prefer nonprofit work environments, which are often more relaxed and less competitive and conventional than mainstream workplaces.

Unfortunately, most jobs at nonprofit organizations pay less than comparable jobs at profit-based companies. However, if salary is not one of your important career values, you can often find nonprofit jobs that are high profile and offer significant responsibility. It might take years to achieve comparable success in the profit-based business world.

Many professional and business organizations, for example Chambers of Commerce, are not profit-making organizations. But, because they are part of the business sector, they are also not true nonprofits in the same way that charitable, religious, education, or conservation organizations are.

A very general test of a true nonprofit is whether contributions to it are tax-deductible. As with every rule, though, there is an exception: Contributions to nonprofits that engage in political lobbying, for example the Sierra Club, cannot be deducted.

NOW YOU KNOW

Newsgroups

There are countless newsgroups that can be extremely useful for job seekers. By searching sites or subscribing to newsgroups related to your personal interests (e.g., anthropology, triathlon competitions, or wildflower gardening), you increase the likelihood of combining your career and your **avocations**—intense interests or activities outside the workplace.

As with other specialty sites, your success at finding a job through newsgroups will vary depending on what you're looking for. Job postings to discussion groups are relatively infrequent, so the odds of finding a position through a discussion group favor those who follow the **threads** (series of messages pertaining to one topic) closely and are knowledgeable about the topic.

Someone who joins a discussion group just to find a job is unlikely to do so any time soon. And posting to a group just to ask about jobs is considered rude and somewhat exploitative, much as if you walked into an acquaintance's house and asked to be served dinner.

If you're a passive job seeker, be *very* careful about using newsgroups to find new jobs. In fact, you may consider avoiding them altogether. Newsgroups are perhaps the most "public" places on the Internet.

What's In It for You?

Specialty sites offer many advantages and disadvantages. Advantages of using specialty sites include:

- **Jobs in all shapes and sizes.** Job seekers can find "ordinary" jobs in interesting or exotic work environments (e.g., an accountant for a dance company or a delivery driver for Amish cabinetmakers).

Some specialty sites will be more useful to you than others. While a visually boring site with a slow search function might list exactly the kinds of jobs you want, a sleek, fun-to-use site might not have content suited to your needs. Remember to bookmark the useful sites and visit them regularly.

❏ *Direct employer contact.* You'll typically receive responses directly from the employer or even a potential supervisor rather than from a third-party recruiter.

❏ *More relevant job listings.* Because specialty sites target a specific segment of the job market, you won't have to weed through as many irrelevant listings as you would on the major job boards.

❏ *Privacy and confidentiality.* You won't need to worry as much about privacy and confidentiality, because so many specialty sites link job seekers directly to the employer.

Disadvantages of using specialty sites include:

❏ *Resume posting.* Compared to the major job boards, a smaller percentage of specialty sites enable you to post your resume, so it is more difficult to be an active job seeker.

❏ *Traffic.* Because there is usually less traffic at specialty sites, fewer potential employers see you.

❏ *Technology.* Most of the specialty sites are less technologically sophisticated than the large job boards, so there is rarely a job search agent to facilitate your search. Many specialty sites have mediocre search functions, sometimes making it difficult to find postings.

❏ *Time.* You must devote more time up front to finding and exploring the sites that best fit your needs.

 Checkpoint

1. Describe three types of employers who might not post jobs on the major commercial job boards.

   _____

   _____

   _____

   _____

2. Why should job seekers who search specialty sites be familiar with comparable jobs posted on the major commercial job boards?

   _____

   _____

   _____

   _____

Search and Respond

Your success in finding jobs through specialty sites depends on the type of job you're searching for. For example, if you are looking for work as a financial analyst for a major corporation, you will almost certainly find more positions on a large job board than on a specialty site. On the other hand, if you are looking for work as a financial analyst for a corporation that is committed to diversity or for a nonprofit public watchdog organization, you might have better luck searching specialty sites.

People whose jobs exist primarily in the nonprofit world, such as fundraising professionals or volunteer and membership coordinators, will greatly expand their job options by searching nonprofit sites and professional and industry associations as well as the major job boards.

Searching for Your Specialty

Your success searching specialty sites also depends on your personality. If you are goal-oriented and like to maximize return for minimal effort, you may find it frustrating to visit a number of niche sites. Before you can search for jobs on specialty sites, you must find the sites themselves. There are a number of ways to do this.

- ❒ Search for the names of associations and organizations you've learned about through school, work, personal interests, or word of mouth.

- ❒ Search **metalists** of professional organizations to find promising sites. Metalists are Web sites or Web pages that provide massive "lists of lists," or links, to a variety of related subjects.

- ❒ Perform basic Web searches using your favorite searching tools.

Using Professional Association Sites

When you visit any professional association site, be sure to search it thoroughly. If you don't see a career link anywhere on the home page, try the site map or headings such as *About Us, Resources, Member Services, Related Sites,* or *Links.* If clicking through the headings doesn't work, practice the following search strategies.

5 STAR WEB SITES

For metalists of professional associations, visit the Internet Public Library Associations on the Net at **www.ipl.org/ref/aon**.

- ❒ Do a site search (if possible) using the keywords *jobs, opportunities,* and *employment.* The jobs may be buried or only accessible through a linked page or site.

- ❒ Be sure to check out the chapter links. A national association that doesn't post jobs may have state or local chapters that do. You may need to search each chapter site individually, but often you'll find links to job boards.

Activity 8.1: Responding to Professional Association Job Listings

To complete this activity, perform an in-depth search for and within professional association sites for job listings that match your career target list. Open the resume documents you created in Chapter 3, and follow the steps below.

1. If possible, find the name of the person who is hiring for the position (through the company Web site or by calling the company).
2. Read the listing to determine which resume format and cover letter format to use.
3. Send your resume and cover letter to the appropriate contact. Print and save e-mailed cover letters for your records.
4. Record the details of each response in a log or a table. A sample record from Carmela follows.

Model Professional Association Response Record

Web Site/Date of Application	Company/Job Title/Date Posted	Contact Information	Type of Resume/ Cover Letter
National Association of Social Workers www.naswdc.org 6/25/20--	Chance Association (Tallahassee, FL) Provides at-risk children with stable homes, positive parenting, and quality education www.chanceassoc.org Residential counselor 6/19/20--	Robert Lafayette President Robertl@chanceassoc. org (850) 555-7709, ext. 4	Electronic personalized resume sent as e-mail attachment Traditional e-mailed cover letter

Using Industry Association Sites

Searching for job listings within industry association sites is similar to searching within professional organization sites.

- ❏ Search sites carefully, and follow any links.

- ❏ If association members are listed, the list may be buried under a subhead that says something like *Consumer Resources*.

- ❏ If the association lists members who maintain Web sites, you're sure to find job listings, but it may take some time to visit all those sites. If you have access to a computer with a fast connection, this would be the time to use it!

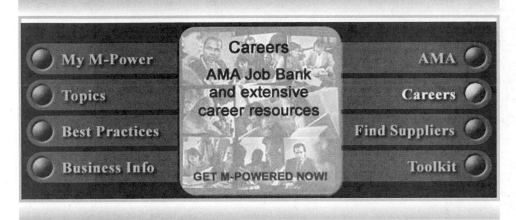

Figure 8.1 Industry Association Site

© 2002 MarketingPower, Inc. (American Marketing Association). Reprinted by permission.

Activity 8.2: Responding to Industry Association Job Listings

To complete this activity, perform an in-depth search for and within professional association sites for job listings that match your career target list. Open the resume documents you created in Chapter 3, and follow the steps below.

1. If possible, find the name of the person who is hiring for the position (through the company Web site or by calling the company).
2. Read the listing to determine which resume format and cover letter format to use.
3. Send your resume and cover letter to the appropriate contact. Print and save e-mailed cover letters for your records.
4. Record the details of each response in a log or a table. A sample record from Carmela follows.

Model Industry Association Response Record

Web Site/Date of Application	Company/Job Title/Date Posted	Contact Information	Type of Resume/ Cover Letter
National Association of Psychiatric Health Systems www.naphs.org 6/25/20--	Cedar Foundation (Austin, TX) Building a healthy community for children www.cedarfoundation. org Mental health associate 6/15/20--	Jarred Bilks Director jarredb@ cedarfoundation.org (512) 555-0500, ext. 18	Electronic personalized resume sent as e-mail attachment Traditional e-mailed cover letter

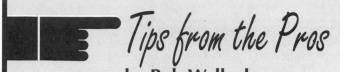

Tips from the Pros

by Bob Wallach
CEO, MarketingPower.com (a subsidiary of the American Marketing Association)
(www.marketingpower.com)

Many industry associations provide extensive job boards and also offer searchable resume databases. Employers often feel that candidates who come through industry association sites, as opposed to the mass-audience job boards (Monster®, HotJobs®, etc.), are a "cut above the rest," since they have taken the extra step of belonging to an association to further their careers and knowledge.

Industry associations also provide an important networking opportunity for job seekers. Association events are wonderful opportunities to meet people who can expand your contacts and provide valuable career advice. Many associations also offer online job fairs, forums, or chat sessions on career-related topics.

If you're new to an association, look for an opportunity to volunteer at an event related to your career interests. By doing so, you'll develop valuable new relationships with other volunteers. You may be asked to recruit (and thereby get to know) prominent speakers, and in some cases you can even MC the event, which is a great way to raise your profile as an industry leader.

Bob Wallach is the creator and CEO of MarketingPower.com, a subsidiary of the American Marketing Association. He earned an MBA with honors from Columbia University and is the recipient of numerous awards, including three Edison New Product Awards and two *BrandWeek* New Product Awards. MarketingPower.com receives approximately 365,000 visitor sessions and 5 million page views each month.

Using Diversity Sites

Even if you are not a member of a minority group, the job listings at many diversity sites can direct you to employers who foster an inclusive workplace. Young workers can also benefit from the workplace preparation content found on many of these sites.

Activity 8.3: Responding to Diversity Site Job Listings

To complete this activity, perform an in-depth search for and within diversity sites for job listings that match your career target list. Open the resume documents you created in Chapter 3, and follow the steps below.

1. If possible, find the name of the person who is hiring for the position (through the company Web site or by calling the company).
2. Read the listing to determine which resume format and cover letter format to use.
3. Send your resume and cover letter to the appropriate contact. Print and save e-mailed cover letters for your records.
4. Record the details of each response in a log or a table. A sample record from Carmela follows.

Model Diversity Site Response Record

Web Site/Date of Application	Company/Job Title/Date Posted	Contact Information	Type of Resume/ Cover Letter
Career Women www.careerwomen. net 6/26/20--	Girl Power (Tallahassee, FL) Shelter for abused and troubled teenage girls www.girlpower.org Full-time residential counselor 6/23/2003	Bonnie Croft Director bcroft@girlpower.org (850) 555-9224, ext. 24	Electronic plain-text resume sent as e-mail text Short e-mailed cover letter

Using Nonprofit Sites

While there are a few comprehensive nonprofit job boards that list opportunities with a variety of organizations, the job seeker who wants employment in the nonprofit sector usually needs a relatively specific idea of where his or her interests lie. For example, if you're looking for work on an organic farm, you could use a nonprofit job board—try Idealist (**www.idealist.org**)—but you would probably have more success using different Internet search techniques to find organic farming associations, individual farms, and educational institutions with organic farming programs.

Activity 8.4: Responding to Nonprofit Site Job Listings

To complete this activity, perform an in-depth search for and within nonprofit sites for job listings that match your career target list. Open the resume documents you created in Chapter 3, and follow the steps below.

1. If possible, find the name of the person who is hiring for the position (through the company Web site or by calling the company).
2. Read the listing to determine which resume format and cover letter format to use.
3. Send your resume and cover letter to the appropriate contact. Print and save e-mailed cover letters for your records.
4. Record the details of each response in a log or a table. A sample record from Carmela is on the next page.

Model Nonprofit Site Response Record

Web Site/Date of Application	Company/Job Title/Date Posted	Contact Information	Type of Resume/ Cover Letter
Nonprofit Career Network www.nonprofitcareer. com 6/26/20--	Smila Center (San Leandro, CA) Provides programs for children ages 3 to 18 with emotional, behavioral, and learning problems www.smila.org Residential counselor 6/18/20--	Joan Capper Human Resources joanc@smila.org (510) 555-1437	Electronic plain-text resume sent as e-mail text Short e-mailed cover letter

Using Newsgroups

Because discussion groups are focused on a particular topic, job openings posted by members are usually a perfect fit for somebody in the group. For example, graduate students studying bat biology might find internships, summer field studies, and other research and job opportunities posted on a discussion group for researchers, educators, and wildlife rehabilitators. A graphic designer who is an avid camper might find a design position with an outdoors magazine posted to her wilderness discussion group.

A number of newsgroups—hosted, for example, by Google™ or Yahoo!®—are not really discussions at all but job listings. These postings are organized by city or state, by career, or by industry. Although some excellent jobs are posted to some of these groups, often by recruiters, you shouldn't confine your search to this method. Be aware that if the group is not moderated by a live person, some of the "jobs" posted are really "easy-money" scams disguised to slip past the content filters.

ETHICS & ETIQUETTE

Wasting other people's time by asking FAQs (frequently asked questions) in a newsgroup is a serious breech of netiquette.

When you join a discussion group, don't ask basic questions you could easily find the answers to elsewhere. That brands you as a "newbie"—an ignorant newcomer. Spend at least a couple of weeks reading posts to get a feel for the general level of discussion. You might not have to ask unnecessary questions if you just keep reading!

Check the legitimacy of the job listings you find using the pointers you've learned in this book. If you find listings that seem legitimate and match your career target list, the newsgroup is worth monitoring. Revisit it every few days to check for new job listings.

Finding a Newsgroup

Newsgroups hosted by Google™, Yahoo!®, or any other large site can be found by clicking on the *Groups* subhead and searching through the Groups directory. You can also search Topica (**www.topica.com**), a large e-mail publisher, the same way. Because these sites host many, many groups, try a number of keyword searches to get the best results.

Finding a newsgroup hosted by a small site is more difficult. Perform several Web search queries, and ask people knowledgeable about the subject if they belong to or know about useful newsgroups.

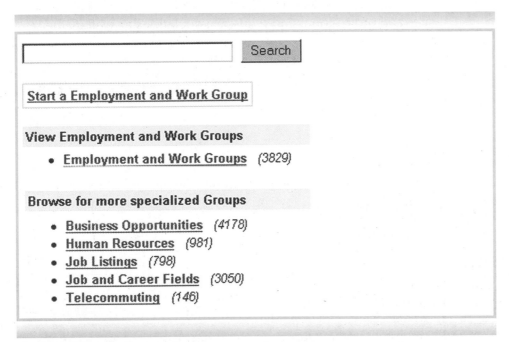

Figure 8.2 Links to Employment Newsgroups

Checkpoint

How can job seekers who are non-minorities benefit from diversity sites?

_____

_____

_____

It's a Wrap

❏ If you have an unusual profession or if you want to work for a small company or nonprofit organization, you might not find the job of your dreams on one of the big job boards. Instead, you should focus your search on the thousands of smaller, specialized job sites, which focus on unique professions and work environments.

❏ Specialty sites have been developed to target certain segments of the job market. There are thousands of specialty sites, and they are as varied as the Internet itself.

❏ People whose jobs exist primarily in the nonprofit world, such as fundraising professionals or volunteer and membership coordinators, will greatly expand their job options by searching nonprofit sites and professional and industry associations as well as the major job boards.

> Whenever it is in any way possible, every boy and girl should choose as his life work some occupation which he should like to do anyhow, even if he did not need the money.
>
> –William Lyon Phelps
> Writer and English professor

Learn the Lingo

Match each term to its definition.

Terms

___ **1.** avocation
___ **2.** industry association
___ **3.** metalists
___ **4.** nonprofit organization
___ **5.** professional association
___ **6.** specialty site
___ **7.** thread

Definitions

a. a Web site that posts job listings for a specialized, or "niche," career field or group

b. an organization of businesses, institutions, or other entities that promotes, and sometimes sets standards for, an industry

c. a series of messages pertaining to one topic

d. an organization that promotes, and sometimes sets standards for, a profession

e. an intense interest or activity outside the workplace

f. a group, agency, or institution whose goals do not include making money

g. Web sites or Web pages that provide massive "lists of lists," or links, to a variety of related subjects

E-valuation

1. Review the job postings you've found on the major job boards and compare them to the job postings you found on specialty sites in this chapter. Write an analysis of your comparison that includes answers to the following questions.

   a. Do the sets differ significantly in number or in kind? If so, how?

   b. Can you make a judgment about which set of jobs is better for you?

   c. Would you mix major boards and specialty sites or rely completely on one kind or another?

   d. Which sites would you visit and how often?

2. Look at your electronic resume in view of the job listings you found at specialty sites. Could you revise your resume to better suit the job descriptions? How?

3. From the job postings you found in this chapter, create a list of five companies that post job opportunities on specialty sites. Now, search for the five companies at some of the major job boards, such as Monster® and HotJobs®. Do the companies also post job opportunities on the major job boards, or do most only post on specialty sites? Based on the results, do you think using specialty sites will help you in your job search? Explain.

"Far and away the best prize that life offers is the chance to work hard at work worth doing."

–Theodore Roosevelt
26th U.S. president

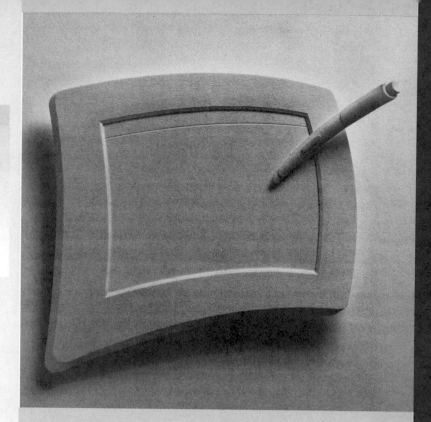

FREELANCING THROUGH THE INTERNET

CHAPTER 9

When embarking on an important purchase or life decision, such as buying a new car or getting married, wise people will tell you to shop around first. If you make an important decision quickly, you risk making the *wrong* decision. Accepting a job offer is one of the most important decisions you'll make in your life. Though most modern workers have many jobs throughout their careers, it's important to understand that *every* job will shape your work experiences, resume, and career path.

If your Internet job search hasn't provided listings that are a perfect or near-perfect match for your career target list, you might consider taking freelance or temporary work until the right thing comes along. In fact, freelancing and temping can often help you find the right thing! This chapter will focus on using the Internet to find freelance and temporary work—alternative paths to traditional, on-site, full-time employment. In addition to valuable information about freelancing and temping job sites, you'll discover the advantages and disadvantages of waiting for the right thing to come along.

Model Job Seeker

Our model job seeker for this chapter is Midori. Midori has just completed her B.A. in graphic design. She has two years of experience as a student worker designing her academic department's newsletters and recruitment brochures. In addition to her work through school, Midori designs CD and vinyl record covers for local musicians. Midori wants to stay in Chicago, and she is reluctant to just take the first position that comes along. Her career target list shows an aptitude for designing magazines, newsletters, advertisements, brochures, book covers, and album covers. She's decided to freelance until she discovers what she likes to do best.

Freelancing: Going It Alone

The most important thing to understand about **freelancing**—working without committing to a particular employer—is that it's not for everyone. It suits some people for a short period of time and others for life. But many people are better off taking advantage of the benefits, regularity, and security an employer can provide.

More and more professionals are getting "off the road"—ditching the daily commute to the office for independence and the comfort of home. E-mail, fax machines, and other modern technologies make freelancing a practical option for many modern workers. And more employers are taking advantage of the larger pool of freelancers for temporary projects and part-time work.

The Advantages

It's not difficult to see why workers are attracted to the concept of freelancing. The "free" aspect of freelancing is what appeals to most people: working at home, choosing your projects, and devising your own work schedule. Advantages of freelancing include:

- ❐ *No daily commute to the office.* Most freelancers don't have to fight rush-hour traffic, and they usually avoid the stress that can come from coworker conflicts and office politics.

- ❐ *Flexible hours.* For the most part, freelancers can set their own hours. If they have children in school, they can start their workdays early. If they're not morning people, they can start their workdays later.

- ❐ *Choosing work.* Freelancers who are good at what they do and have a lot of contacts can pick and choose the work that suits them. And they always have the option of declining work.

The Disadvantages

While the freedom and independence gained from freelancing can be a welcome change from the daily office routine, that freedom comes with extra responsibilities. Disadvantages of freelancing include:

- ❐ *No paid company benefits.* Freelancers don't receive the benefits typically associated with working for one employer, such as health insurance, paid holidays, sick leave, and vacation days.

- ❐ *No support from coworkers.* If freelancers have a computer problem or need answers to specific questions, they're on their own. Many freelancers also miss the companionship of coworkers, including face-to-face interactions and office friendships.

❏ *Time management and home distractions.* Working from home takes *a lot* of self-discipline. Freelancers must be able to motivate themselves, manage their time well, and avoid distractions such as housework, children, and television.

❏ *Finances.* Freelancers buy their own office supplies, pay for monthly Internet service, and purchase or maintain any other major office needs. And most clients will not withhold taxes, so freelancers need to plan ahead and keep detailed records.

Consulting

If you're a senior-level executive or have a lot of experience in your career field, you might consider **consulting**—being paid to give expert advice on a particular subject. Consultants are hired when a company needs help with a process, service, or system. Consultants work in telecommunications, networking, human resources, landscaping, interior design, and just about any other field you can imagine. While consulting is similar to freelancing from home, there are some differences.

❏ Though consultants are typically based at home, their work often requires them to travel to other locations.

❏ Consultants are usually paid at much higher rates than freelancers are.

❏ Consultants are responsible for larger outcomes, such as the success of a company-wide billing system or the safety of a playground.

❏ Consultants have more difficulty finding job postings online and, therefore, must work harder to find clients (e.g., by setting up a professional Web site or calling contacts directly).

Checkpoint

1. List three additional advantages and disadvantages to freelancing.

_____

_____

_____

2. How is consulting similar to freelancing? How does it differ?

_____

_____

_____

Temping: Shopping Around

Temping—working for an agency that provides on-site temporary workers to various employers—can be a great way to earn money while exploring different work environments and job titles. If you don't mind moving from place to place or being thrown into unfamiliar work environments, temping might be the work for you.

Temping is also a great way to add skills to your resume and make business contacts. If you're fortunate, it can also lead to permanent employment. You could even land a permanent job with one of your target companies by temping for them first.

How Temping Works

Traditionally, temporary agencies have provided employees for office or light industrial positions that open temporarily because of employee absence or a company's need to produce more work in a short period of time. Temporary employees work for and are paid by the temporary agency, not the company that has the work.

For example, an administrative assistant who signs up with a temporary agency will be assigned to different jobs as they become available. He might work in three different offices in one week or in one office for a few weeks (to relieve someone who is on extended leave or to help the company through a busy time).

The New Offerings

Temporary agencies have grown substantially in recent years and now tend to offer general employment services as well as traditional temporary assignments. In fact, many have scrapped the term *temporary*, preferring to call themselves *employment services* or *personnel services*. In addition to traditional temporary assignments, many temporary agencies offer:

- ❏ *One-time, long-term contracts.* For example, a company that needs a Java programmer to create an elaborate new Web site expects the project to take seven months but won't necessarily have work for the programmer when the project is finished.

- ❏ *Permanent full-time job listings.* Some temporary agencies now work like third-party recruiters. They list full-time openings and are paid by the hiring company to find suitable candidates.

- ❏ *Temp-to-hire jobs.* Countless employees have been burned by accepting a permanent job that was not all it was cracked up to be. Employers have been burned as well by hiring employees who don't quite live up to their interviews. That's why more and more employers are offering "temp-to-hire" jobs as a way of screening potential employees for full-time positions. After a period of time, if the temporary employee likes the job and the employer likes the employee, the situation is made permanent.

Advantages

Flexibility, experience, pay—the benefits of temping are numerous. Temporary employees:

- ❑ Receive a regular paycheck with taxes withheld.
- ❑ Get to try out a variety of work environments.
- ❑ Make new contacts in different career fields and at different companies.
- ❑ Gain new experience and work skills.
- ❑ Are sometimes eligible for benefits, such as health insurance or a retirement plan, through the temporary agency.
- ❑ Often find a good match for a permanent job.

Disadvantages

Like freelancing and telecommuting, temping isn't for everyone. Some people, for example, don't like to be thrown into unfamiliar situations day after day. Temporary employees:

- ❑ Can't always find temping work in their career fields.
- ❑ Must deal with constantly changing, sometimes disagreeable, work environments.
- ❑ Are frequently expected to take on the more unpleasant or menial tasks in an office.

Checkpoint

1. How do "temp-to-hire" jobs benefit both employees and employers?

_____

_____

2. Are you a good candidate for temporary work? Why or why not?

_____

_____

Freelancing and Temping Job Sites

Any person who has chosen an alternative path—one that breaks away from a traditional approach—can tell you that it's rarely easy. Likewise, conducting a search for "nontraditional" freelance and temp jobs may be one of the most challenging parts of an Internet job search.

Though the Internet offers many Web sites dedicated to providing freelance and temporary job listings, these sites don't post many true "freelancing" jobs—jobs that allow you to work completely off site. Odd as it may seem, freelancing sites can be a great resource for permanent job seekers. If you're serious about finding freelancing or temp work online, however, you'll need to increase your patience and determination.

Freelancing Sites

Like company Web sites and newsgroups, freelancing job sites vary greatly according to types of postings, number of postings, search functions, and complexity. Freelancing job sites come in two main varieties.

- ❑ **Traditional freelancing sites** are freelancing job sites that work like job boards. They house job seeker resume banks and employer job banks. Some, however, offer job listings only.

- ❑ **Job bidding sites** are freelancing job sites that work like online auctions. Site users bid on freelance project listings by assessing the job and submitting a price for doing the work.

Traditional Freelancing Sites

Traditional freelancing sites can be unfriendly to the job seeker for several reasons. In addition to unrefined search engines and limited job postings, many sites charge monthly or annual member fees to access listings or assess fees for commissions. And many offer freelancing jobs that are actually on-site contract jobs, which means you can't do them from home!

The following traditional freelancing sites are worth visiting.

- ❑ Guru®: **www.guru.com**
- ❑ Freelance Online: **www.freelanceonline.com**
- ❑ ContractJobHunter: **www.cjhunter.com**
- ❑ Creative Freelancers: **www.freelancers.com**
- ❑ Workaholics4Hire.com: **www.workaholics4hire.com**
- ❑ Telecommuting Jobs™: **www.tjobs.com**

NOW YOU KNOW

While paying for anything related to getting a *particular* job (e.g., paying for supplies or training as a condition of employment) is always a bad idea, paying for an employment *service,* such as access to job listings specific to your career field, can be beneficial.

Paying Fees

Annual fees for viewing freelancing site job postings typically range from $10 to $50 per year. Those that assess larger fees often offer a smaller monthly rate for job seekers who don't want to commit to a full year.

Before you pay a fee, research the job site thoroughly. If the site will not allow you to view a sample of listings without joining, call them and ask specific questions about the types of listings offered, including career fields, locations, and the number of new listings per week. Ask for references from satisfied freelancers. Trust your instincts! If the responses are vague or the company is not very helpful, don't give them your money.

Read the Fine Print

Often, a site will collect a commission on the work you perform. It is the site's right to do so, and it is not necessarily a harmful practice. However, a wise freelancer should know how each site's payment system works. Read, print, and save the Web site's legal information concerning fees, commissions, and job seekers' rights and responsibilities.

Location Considerations

You may be wondering why location matters at all if you're working from home! While some freelancers may never meet their clients face-to-face, many clients who offer longer-term contracts prefer to hire a freelancer who is located nearby and can attend the occasional in-house meeting. And many clients advertise on-site contract work on freelancing job sites. Read freelance job postings carefully. A true off-site freelance job will have no location specifications whatsoever.

Job Bidding Sites

In addition to posting jobs for auction, job bidding sites allow job seekers to post their resumes in online databases. So even if you don't get the bid, you might be contacted for a project that isn't listed on the site. Another advantage to using job bidding sites is accessibility: They typically don't charge job seekers for viewing their listings.

The following job bidding sites are worth visiting.

- ❒ ePlaced.com: **www.eplaced.com**
- ❒ eLance™: **www.elance.com**
- ❒ Contracted Work: **www.contractedwork.com**
- ❒ Monster® Contract & Temporary: **http://talentmarket. monster.com**

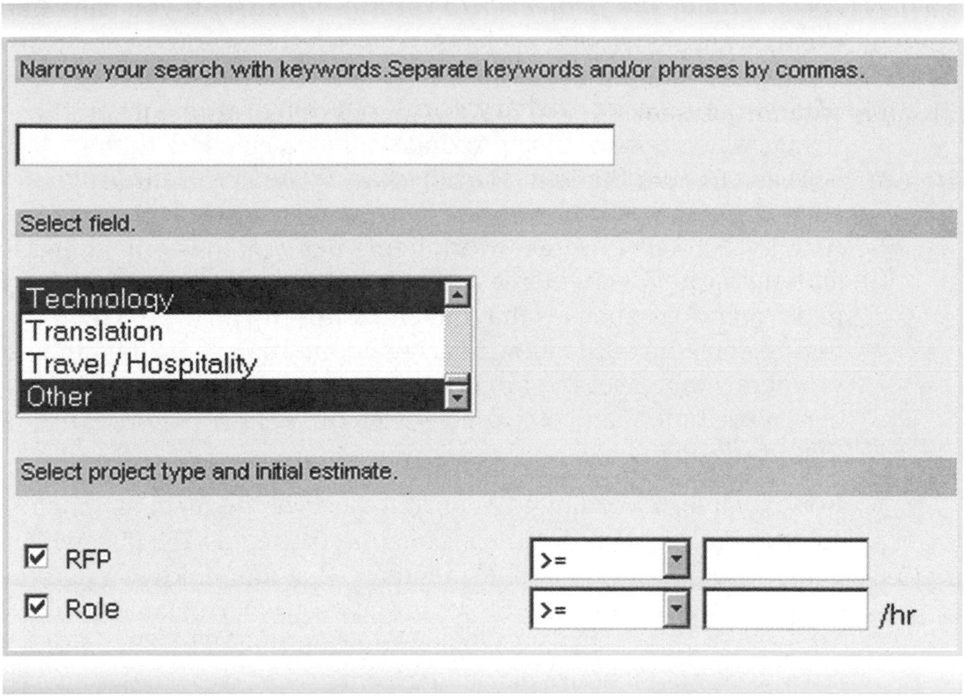

Figure 9.1 Job Bidding Site Search Fields

Assessing Job Costs

Clients will typically offer a flat amount for an entire freelance project (e.g., $1,500 for designing a brochure, or $18,000 for writing a computer program). Most clients will allow you to send **invoices** (written records of goods or services provided and the amount charged for them that are sent to a customer as requests for payment) as you complete phases of the project. Sometimes, clients either aren't sure about what to charge or don't want to offer a figure that is too high. Whether the client offers a flat amount at the outset or asks you how much you charge, you should:

- ❐ *Assess the project before you offer a price.* Clients frequently push to agree upon a figure before you've had time to evaluate how much time the project will take and what will be asked of you. Let the client know you are interested and ask for a day or two to figure out what the project is worth.

- ❐ *Research payments for similar projects.* Look at one of the freelance job sites (you'll research these sites in depth later in this chapter), such as eLance™ (**www.elance.com**), and try to find similar projects. Ask professionals from your career field what they would charge for the project. Though the figures will vary greatly based on deadline and scope, you should be able to come up with a rough estimate.

> **NOW YOU KNOW**
>
> When negotiating payment for a project, don't undercharge clients! Many clients assume that a higher quote promises better work. You may lose some jobs from charging too much, but you may also lose some from charging too little. Expect a fair price for your work, and never go beneath your minimum hourly rate.

❐ **Break down the project into an hourly rate.** If you can't find price quotes for similar projects, research the average or median salary for professionals in your field and location. Try Salary.com™ (**www.salary.com**), but don't rely solely on the result, which is only an approximation; also check with the Bureau of Labor Statistics' *Occupational Outlook Handbook* (**www.bls.gov/oco**). Divide the average salary you come up with by 2,080 (the average work hours per year) to come up with an hourly rate. Then, increase that hourly rate by 30 to 50 percent to account for expenses that the client doesn't provide. When you've come up with a new hourly rate, multiply it by the number of hours you expect the project to take. Always add about 10 percent more time than you expect—something always comes up that you didn't plan for!

For example, according to Midori's research, the median annual salary for a graphic design specialist in Chicago is $43,000, which equates to $21 per hour. She'll increase that amount by 40 percent to $29 per hour. Therefore, for a two-week freelance project, Midori will charge $2,552: $29 per hour multiplied by 88 hours (two weeks at 80 hours plus 10 percent).

Earnings   [About this section] ▲ Top

Earnings for desktop publishers vary according to level of experience, training, location, and size of firm. Median annual earnings of desktop publishers were $30,600 in 2000. The middle 50 percent earned between $22,890 and $40,210. The lowest 10 percent earned less than $17,800, and the highest 10 percent earned more than $50,920 a year. Median annual earnings in the industries employing the largest numbers of these workers in 2000 are shown below:

Commercial printing	$30,940
Newspapers	24,520

Related Occupations   [About this section] ▲ Top

Desktop publishers use artistic and editorial skills in their work. These skills also are essential for <u>artists and related workers</u>; <u>designers</u>; <u>news analysts, reporters, and correspondents</u>; <u>public relations specialists</u>; <u>writers and editors</u>; and <u>prepress technicians and workers</u>.

Figure 9.2 Entry from the Occupational Outlook Handbook
©2002. Used with permission of the author.

Tips from the Pros

by Bradford Rand
Founder and CEO, Job Expo International, Inc.
(www.job-expo.com)

Strategies for Job Fair Attendees

Research the hiring event before you go. Most job fairs have Web sites that list the participating companies and their available positions. You may also be able to use the Web site to set up interviews in advance, giving you a head start over the other job seekers.

Be prepared. Get a good night's sleep—you'll need the extra energy to handle what amounts to numerous short interviews in a few hours time.

Don't be limited to the jobs listed in the program guide. Most job fairs advertise hundreds of available positions, but you should also inquire about positions that have not been advertised.

Take advantage of networking opportunities. You may meet people who know of jobs that fit your skills or can forward your resume to another division or department of their company. In addition, you may meet people who have been in situations similar to yours and can offer advice.

Broaden your career horizons. Use career expos to learn about different types of positions, including ones you hadn't considered before. Meet with companies you thought you'd never work for; you might like what the company has to offer, and, even if you don't, it's good practice for when you meet with your dream company.

Bradford Rand is the founder and CEO of Job Expo International, Inc., one of the leading career event producers for over 10 years. The job fairs his company produces include JOBEXPO for sales and management professionals (www.job-expo.com), TECHEXPO for computer professionals (www.techexpousa.com), HealthExpo for healthcare, biotech, and pharmaceutical professionals (www.healthexpousa.com), and DiversityExpo for companies hiring with equal opportunity in mind (www.diversityexpo.com).

Source: Bureau of Labor Statistics

Activity 9.1: Freelancing Job Site Search and Evaluation

Using your Web searching strategies, find at least three freelancing sites specific to your career field and location. You can include the major job boards if you like. On a separate piece of paper, organize the sites you've found into a table. An example from Midori's search is provided to guide you.

Model List of Freelancing Sites

Web Site Name and URL	Traditional or Bidding Site?	Type of Listings	Fees/Other Comments
AF Work www.allfreelancework.com	Major portal to several freelance sites	Many job types and locations	Free registration; fee for adding a profile and resume
Contracted Work www.contractedwork.com	Bidding site	Extensive listings; lots of interesting design projects	No fees
Guru www.guru.com	Traditional site	Limited listings	No fees; charges employer flat fee for successful placement. Service is free for small employers with short-term contracts.

Online Work-At-Home Scams

Make $1,000 a week processing medical insurance claims. Turn your computer into a cash machine. You've seen these advertisements in the printed newspapers. Now, they're popping up everywhere online. In fact, when you conduct your freelancing site search, you're bound to find them. When you find these sites online, pay attention. Closely examine offers that guarantee income from work-at-home programs, and remember this rule: If it *sounds* too good to be true, it probably *is*.

5 STAR WEB SITES

To find out if an online work-from-home offer is legitimate, visit the Better Business Bureau's Web site dedicated to work-at-home schemes at **www.bbb.org/library/workathome.asp**. The Mom's Work at Home Site offers 10 tips for avoiding work-at-home scams. Check out the tips and other advice at **www.momsworkathomesite.com/scams.htm**.

Tips for Spotting Scams
If you've found an offer that you're not sure is legitimate, watch for the following "scam giveaways."

❐ There is no real job description.

❐ The site is like a continual loop: Every time you click to get some more information, it's just more of the same promotional text.

❐ The end of your loop is always a book or guide that you must pay for.

Work-at-Home Scams from the Better Business Bureau
The Better Business Bureau, a government agency that protects consumers from fraud, has identified common work-at-home scams, many of which cost job seekers thousands of dollars. The Better Business Bureau warns job seekers to be aware of the following work-at-home scams.

❐ *Assembly work at home:* This scam requires you to pay for craft assembly instructions and materials. After you've assembled the products, the company often decides not to pay you, claiming that the work has not met "standards."

❏ *Envelope stuffing:* These ads promise a weekly salary for stuffing envelopes from home. Most people who answer the ads never receive the envelopes or the stuffing materials! Instead, they receive promotional materials that promise proven money-making plans. Job seekers who pay for the money-making plans receive instructions for placing ads similar to the ones they responded to.

❏ *Computer-related work:* Most of these ads promise lots of money for using your home computer for word-processing, data entry, or other computer-related work. You wind up paying for a worthless computer disk or a guide to work-at-home jobs, which lists either government Web sites that you can find yourself or business opportunities that require more money.

❏ *Processing medical insurance claims:* Job seekers who respond to these ads are pressured to buy software programs, computers, and (probably phony) training at ridiculously high costs. Once they've put out money and time, they're often told that there is a backlog in processing pay or that their work has "mistakes."

Temping Sites

Temporary agencies work as third-party recruiters for employers who need help finding candidates for short-term work or temp-to-hire jobs. They hire temporary workers and then sell those workers' services to various employers.

Before you begin your search for temporary work, there are some important things to know about temping sites.

❏ Temping agencies don't always list their job openings on their Web sites. Many agencies prefer to meet you in person.

❏ In order to apply for job listings online, you must submit a resume.

❏ If an agency doesn't exist in your desired location, the listings won't be useful to you.

❏ Temping sites also provide some permanent job listings.

The following temping sites are worth visiting.

❏ Net-Temps®: **www.net-temps.com**

❏ JobListings.net: **www.joblistings.net**

❏ Kelly Services®: **www.kellyservices.com**

☐ Manpower®: **www.manpower.com**

☐ Manpower® Professional:
   www.manpowerprofessional.com

☐ OfficeTeam®: **www.officeteam.com**

Activity 9.2: Temping Job Site Search and Evaluation

Find at least three temping sites specific to your career field and location. Even if you want permanent work or short-term jobs to supplement your freelancing, these sites may provide what you're looking for. Midori, for example, is looking for short-term (2-3 days in length) graphic design positions until she builds up her freelancing contacts. On a separate piece of paper, organize the sites you've found into a table. An example from Midori's search is provided to guide you.

Model List of Temping Sites

Web Site Name and URL	Type of Listings
Manpower Professional www.manpowerprofessional.com	No current listings for graphic designers
Kelly Services www.kellyservices.com	One listing for a technical illustrator
Net-Temps www.net-temps.com	Three listings for graphic designers, but contracts are probably too long
JobListings.net www.joblistings.net	One listing for a graphic designer, but contract is too long

Checkpoint

1. In your own words, explain the difference between a traditional freelancing site and a job bidding site.

_____

_____

_____

2. Have you encountered any scams similar to those listed on the Better Business Bureau's Web site? Explain.

_____

_____

_____

It's a Wrap

☐ If your Internet job search hasn't provided listings that are a perfect or near-perfect match for your career target list, you might consider taking freelance or temporary work until the right thing comes along.

☐ E-mail, fax machines, and other modern technologies make freelancing a practical option for many modern workers.

☐ If you don't mind moving from place to place or being thrown into unfamiliar work environments, temping might be the work for you.

☐ Conducting a search for "nontraditional" freelance and temp jobs may be one of the most challenging parts of an Internet job search.

Learn the Lingo

Match each term to its definition.

Terms

___ 1. consulting
___ 2. freelancing
___ 3. invoice
___ 4. job bidding site
___ 5. temping
___ 6. traditional freelancing site

Definitions

a. working for an agency that provides on-site temporary workers to various employers

b. working without committing to a particular employer

c. being paid to give expert advice on a particular subject

d. a freelancing job site that works like an online auction

e. a freelancing job site that works like a job board

f. a written record of goods or services provided and the amount charged for them that is sent to a customer as a request for payment

E-valuation

1. Use the Internet to find professional opinions about what it takes to become a successful freelancer. Look for articles and professional freelancing organizations. Compile a list of attributes. How many of these attributes do you have?

2. Find six work-from-home job listings. Do they appear to be genuine? Explain. Visit **www.bbb.org** and search for information about each of the listings. How accurate were your assessments?

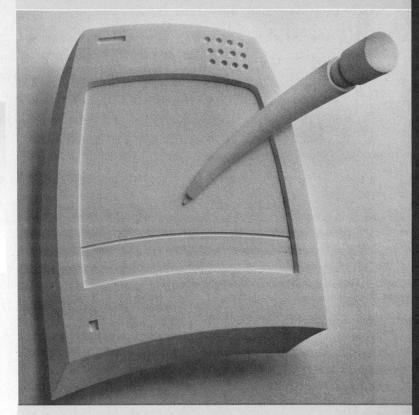

CHAPTER 10

CHAPTER OBJECTIVES

- ❏ Learn to monitor and generate more responses from your online resume.
- ❏ Discover ways to effectively handle responses to your resume, including phone contact, e-mail contact, and interviews.

REFINING YOUR INTERNET JOB SEARCH

If you've ever plugged in a string of old holiday lights only to find that they won't light, you understand how difficult it can be to get to the root of a problem. To find what's causing the trouble, you must unscrew each light, *one by one*. If you're not getting the responses you expected from your Internet job search or you're getting responses but not clinching the deal, you may be wondering where and how you've gone wrong. Fortunately, there are better ways to find the "broken light" in your Internet job search.

In fact, it's quite easy to monitor and refine your Internet job search based on your results. This chapter provides strategies for finding and fixing common Internet job search problems—from increasing low responses to handling those responses effectively. Even if you've fared well throughout your search, you'll discover career tools you can use for life.

Model Job Seeker

Our model job seeker for this chapter is Joshua, a telecommunications major from Canton, Ohio, who has worked as an intern in LAN/WAN network engineering for three summers. Joshua is looking for entry-level positions in data communications engineering and wants to stay in or near Canton. Joshua hasn't received as many responses from his online resume as he'd hoped. And, though his direct responses to online job postings have generated a few phone calls and one interview, he still hasn't been offered a position. Joshua's experiences with refining his Internet job search are provided as examples throughout this chapter.

Getting Responses

There are two basic phases in any job search: getting responses from recruiters and handling those responses. Traditional job seekers have often experienced difficulty diagnosing problems that occur in the first phase. The Internet, however, makes it much easier to discover why you might not be getting the responses you desire.

If your Internet job search hasn't generated many responses that match your career target list, don't lose hope! There are several things you can do to get that phone ringing.

Monitoring Your Resume Views

Many job boards provide statistics about how many recruiters have viewed your resume—how many **views** your resume has received. The term *view* may refer to different things depending on the job board's definition, but it typically means that your resume summary has appeared in a recruiter's search results. This feature is an extremely useful tool for monitoring your resume activity.

Even if your resume received a view, it didn't necessarily receive a **detailed view**, which occurs when a recruiter goes one step further by reviewing your complete resume. Most job boards that provide statistics about resume views make a distinction between *views* and *detailed views*.

Analyzing Views

If your resume isn't generating many views, the problem most likely lies with your use of keywords. Recruiters search databases for resumes with specific keywords. If your resume doesn't include those keywords, it won't get a view. If your resume is generating a lot of views but very few detailed views, your keywords may be too general and your resume may be appearing as a match for jobs that have nothing to do with your career field.

How many detailed views should your resume generate? It depends on how many initial views your resume generates. For example, an IT professional with target locations in big cities may receive five times as many initial views as a job seeker who is looking for work as a dental hygienist in a smaller town. That IT professional should also expect to have more detailed views. With detailed views, however, overall percentage is more meaningful than total numbers. Your total detailed views should be between 9 and 15 percent of your total views. If your total detailed views aren't at least 8 percent of your total views, you should strongly consider modifying the content of your resume.

NOW YOU KNOW

Think of resume views as a way to gauge the overall success of your Internet job search. Even if your job search is not centered around the major job boards, analyzing your resume views can give you a general picture of how recruiters are responding to your resume.

Activity 10.1: Find Your Detailed View Percentage

To figure out your detailed view percentage, divide the number of detailed views by the total number of views. For example, Joshua's CareerBuilder® resume has generated 15 views and 1 detailed view. So he's divided 1 by 15 to get .06, or 6 percent.

Model Detailed View Percentage

Job Board	Total Views	Total Detailed Views	Detailed View Percentage
CareerBuilder	15	1	6%
Monster	28	2	7%
HotJobs	18	1	5.5%

Your Detailed View Percentage

Job Board	Total Views	Total Detailed Views	Detailed View Percentage

Revising Your Keywords

When recruiters perform an initial keyword search, they get long lists of potential candidates and a brief section of each candidate's resume, which is typically the summary of qualifications (keyword summary) and/or objective. When you come up in that list, it registers as a view.

The recruiters then review each resume summary and/or objective and use that information to decide whether your resume is worth a closer look. If it is, they look over your entire resume (work experience, degrees, etc.). When that happens, it registers as a detailed view.

Though *every* aspect of your resume must impress recruiters, your keywords can make or break your chances at getting detailed views. Search results are displayed in order of the number of keyword matches, so if your resume has more matches, it will be higher on the list. Since recruiters have limited time to review resumes, most will focus on the first few on the list, which is where you want your resume to be.

Activity 10.2: Revising Your Objective and Summary of Qualifications

Because Joshua's detailed view percentage is less than 8 percent on all the major job boards, he's decided to revise his objective and summary of qualifications by using more career-related keywords. (Refer to Chapter 3 before you revise your objective or keyword summary.)

Model Revised Objective and Summary of Qualifications

Objective: To obtain a position in telecommunications engineering, data communications engineering, or LAN/WAN network engineering.

Summary of Qualifications: Data communications engineer with experience supporting LAN/WAN network infrastructures for large companies. Experienced in specifications, procurements, and implementation of LAN/WAN network topology, diagnostics, equipment, and connectivity. Technical background includes Cisco routers and switches, TCP/IP, DLSW, IPX security, and firewalls.

Your Revised Objective and Summary of Qualifications

Objective:

Summary of Qualifications:

Revising Your Resume

If you're receiving plenty of views and detailed views, but the phone isn't ringing, your resume is probably in need of a general review. Your resume should be well crafted, be free of grammatical errors and typos, and properly reflect your career goals and experiences. To ensure your resume isn't scaring recruiters away:

❏ *Give it a peer review.* Ask two people (friends, family members, teachers, coworkers, etc.) with successful job-hunting experience to read your resume and offer suggestions for improvement. Make sure you squelch the urge to overrule critical suggestions. Many job seekers guard their resumes like prized possessions but forget that, like all other prized possessions, resumes occasionally need to be appraised and restored.

❏ ***Create more resume versions.*** Even within career fields, job titles and responsibilities can vary greatly. And your career target list might include slightly different job titles. Unless you can expect to encounter the same requirements for every job you apply to, it's a good idea to have more than one resume version. For example, a technology engineer might have two resume versions—one focusing on software skills and one focusing on hardware skills.

Give your resume versions descriptive names so that you always know which one you're sending. If the jobs you're applying for vary in scope, consider posting more than one resume version in the online resume databases.

❏ ***Check your terminology.*** As you know, career-related keywords are the ticket to generating "first looks" at your resume. In addition to putting you on the list of potential candidates, using the language of your career field indicates that you are knowledgeable about the industry. Incorporate several practical, specific statements that demonstrate your grasp of the field, but be careful not to overuse or abuse technical terms. If a human resources professional cannot decipher your work experience, this technique can work against you.

5 STAR WEB SITES

Feeling frustrated by rejections or a lack of response to your resume? Lighten your mood with one job seeker's take on the infamous rejection letter at **www.rileyguide.com/reject.html**

If you're having trouble determining the best keywords to include, try the following: Find 10 job listings that closely match your ideal position based on the job title, industry, and level of experience required. Make a list of the keywords used in the listings. Then analyze your list: Look for common keywords among the listings. Recruiters often search for the same keywords they use in their job listings, so add any common keywords you find to your resume.

❏ ***Rewrite your objective.*** If your objective doesn't clearly state your career goal, including the industry and job title of the position you're looking for, recruiters may not be reading any farther. If you're searching for more than one job title or in more than one industry, create different resume versions, each one with a specific objective.

Resume Writing Services

A growing number of job seekers are utilizing the services of professional resume writers. A professional resume writing service can be a powerful tool or a complete waste of time and money. The results you get depend on the firm you use and the qualifications of the writer who prepares your resume. The fees for resume writing services, which typically range from $100 to $1,000, vary significantly based on the service provider and your career level.

Never pay for a professional resume writing service without researching the company, viewing examples, and checking references. Before you choose a service, ask the following questions.

- ❑ *What qualifications do your writers have?* The resume writers will have your livelihood in their hands—make sure they're up to the task.

- ❑ *What guarantees do you offer?* Any reputable service will at least guarantee to rewrite your resume for free if you're not getting results.

- ❑ *Will I be able to communicate directly with the writer?* A vital part of a resume writing service is communication with the writer. If a service won't allow you to discuss your career goals and experiences with the writer, you should keep looking for one that will.

Resume "Blasting" Services

Another e-recruiting resource that has gained some traction is **resume "blasting"**—using a fee-based service to send your resume via fax or e-mail to thousands of companies and/or third-party recruiters. Resume blasting services provide a broadcast service for your resume. Some provide a larger database of contacts, and some provide better targeting capabilities, but they all send your resume to the types of search firms and employers that you are targeting.

The convenience these services provide is apparent: Your resume is sent to thousands of contacts in a very short period of time—all without much effort and usually for less than $200. But not all services actually do what they promise. Some don't send your resume directly to a recruiter. Instead, they may send it to a company's resume intake system. Some services don't even go that far. They store your resume in electronic mailboxes created for recruiters. Recruiters who don't take the initiative to retrieve the resumes will never even see yours.

Bulk Job Board Registration Services

A new service being offered is bulk job board registration. The providers register you on many different job boards with a single registration. Using one of these services will definitely save you time, but the results may not be worth it. Different job boards require different formatting, organization, and sometimes even information. If you don't take the time to register individually at each site, your resulting profile may not accurately reflect your objectives and experience.

5 STAR WEB SITES

For lists of screened, reviewed, and ranked resume writing and blasting services, visit the Web site for this book at
www.jobseekersecrets.com

Tips from the Pros

by Dan Cahn
Founder, WorkLife Solutions, Inc.
(www.worklife.com)

When the economy is tight and there are more applicants than positions, job seekers may be tempted to purchase services, such as resume writing, interview training, or resume blasting, to help them land the job. These services can be an invaluable addition to your job search, but you should do some homework before investing in them. Otherwise, you could wind up with an offer that really is too good to be true. Before spending money on a service, answer the following questions.

- Is the service offered by a reputable Web site? Are credible testimonials provided?

- Will the service increase your chances of finding a job? Job seekers are often better served by networking and targeting specific companies.

- What guarantee, if any, does the site offer? Will they refund your money or provide additional services if you don't find a job in a specific time period?

People pay lawyers, accountants, and financial advisors, but seldom invest in personal career professionals. The return on that investment, if it is made wisely, can be lifelong.

Dan Cahn is a 20+ year career expert, former employment and training federal executive, a founder of Projects to Assist Employment, a partner in Mainstream Access, Inc., and a founder of WorkLife Solutions, Inc., a 10-year-old online career development organization.

Checkpoint

1. In your own words, explain the difference between a view and a detailed view.

_____

_____

_____

2. List and explain three ways to revise your resume for better results.

_____

_____

_____

3. What should you look for in a professional resume writing service?

_____

_____

_____

Handling Responses

The stage is set. You've posted your resume online and applied directly to job listings through companies and third-party recruiters. Lights! Camera! Job offer! If only it were that easy. While the Internet will greatly increase your prospects, it won't get you out of handling responses to your resume.

If your Internet job search has generated plenty of views, detailed views, and calls from employers and you're still not getting on-site interviews, you might need to improve your telephone and e-mail communication with recruiters during the pre-interview screening.

Telephone Contact

Sometimes an employer will be so impressed by your resume that you'll be called directly to set up an on-site interview. Often, however, the first call from an employer is yet another screening process—a "mini" interview that helps an employer decide whether to invite you in for the real thing.

Your first phone contact from an employer might be:

- ❐ A call from a human resources professional or administrative assistant instead of the person who has the authority to hire you. The caller will either set up an interview with the hiring manager or ask you a few questions to gauge your professionalism, personality, and interest in the position. Beware: Many hiring managers ask employees to narrow down a stack of resumes by eliminating candidates over the phone.

- ❐ A call from the hiring manager (your potential boss). He or she might directly ask to set up an interview, ask a few quick questions to decide whether or not to invite you in, or perform a more in-depth, "mini" interview over the phone. Phone interviews can last as long as 30 minutes, so you'll want to be prepared!

Getting "Phone-Ready"

There are several things you can do to be ready for phone contact from employers. The time it takes to prepare is well worth the reward.

- ❐ Make sure your outgoing phone message sounds professional. If you live with roommates or young children, you might consider adding a second line until you find employment. Let your answering machine or voicemail take a call when you're not prepared.

- ❐ Let everyone in your household know that you are expecting calls from potential employers, and ask them to answer the phone professionally and take detailed messages.

> "Thorough preparation makes its own luck."
>
> –Joe Poyer
> American writer/novelist

☐ Keep materials by the phone, such as your resumes, cover letters, job application logs, individual company research, and responses to common interview questions. Keep a pen and paper handy as well.

☐ Practice responding to common interview questions and role-play your phone conversation with a friend. You might want to use a tape recorder so that you can evaluate and improve your performance.

Acing the Telephone Interview

Some employers will warn you in advance about a longer phone interview. Others won't because they want to test your thinking and communication skills by putting you on the spot. If an employer calls and wants to do a phone interview right away, excuse yourself politely and offer to call back in five minutes. It's best not to offer a reason. Decent employers should understand the need to be composed. To sail through your phone interview:

☐ *Create your interview setting.* Find a quiet place where you can talk without interruptions. Get rid of distractions, such as music, television, pets, roommates, and family. Disable call waiting. Have a glass of water handy to avoid coughing spells.

☐ *Write down the essentials.* Record any information that is essential to the interview, such as the interviewer's name and details about the position. Refer specifically to that information throughout the interview to show you're paying attention.

☐ *Be brief.* Answer each question concisely, giving no more or no less than asked. This interviewing rule of thumb is especially important during phone interviews. The lack of visual cues makes it difficult to determine when the interviewer is ready to move to the next question. If you're not sure you've said enough, end your responses with a question, such as, *"Would you like more details about my experiences with LAN/WAN networks?"*

☐ *Be professional.* It should go without saying, but some interviewees still make the mistake of treating the interviewer like a casual friend. This rule applies to third-party recruiters as well! Though you don't want to come off as rigid or robotic, always err on the side of professionalism, especially during phone interviews. Humor from both sides can be misinterpreted when visual cues are not available.

☐ *Let the employer end the interview.* Unless your house is on fire, never end the interview yourself. Let the employer finish asking all questions, thank the interviewer for his or her time, and restate your interest in the position.

E-Mail Contact

Though most employers prefer to call you directly, some will contact you by e-mail. E-mail contact from an employer is typically similar to phone contact: It will either come from a human resources professional or directly from the hiring manager, and it may range from a quick invitation for an on-site interview to a longer list of questions. When responding to employers through e-mail:

☐ Follow all rules concerning professionalism and brevity. Apply the same guidelines to writing business e-mails as you would to any professional document.

☐ Avoid using all capital letters. In the electronic world, it's equivalent to shouting.

☐ Avoid using **emoticons** (an acronym for *emotion icons;* small icons composed of punctuation characters that indicate the sender's emotion). Smiley faces are fine between friends and family but not so fine when addressing an employer.

☐ Write short, concise sentences.

☐ Use proper greetings and salutations.

☐ Parse separate ideas into paragraphs, and avoid rambling or run-on sentences.

☐ Check for correct spelling and grammar.

Activity 10.3: Preparing for Interview Questions

Interview questions serve a number of purposes. Some are designed to determine what you know about the position, and some are designed to determine what kind of person you are. When answering interview questions, be brief, be honest, never argue, and always turn negatives into positives. Practice answering the following common interview questions.

1. Why are you interested in this job?
2. Describe the responsibilities of your current or previous position.
3. What do you know about this industry?
4. Why do you think you would like to work for our company?
5. What is your most significant accomplishment?
6. Why did you leave your last job?
7. How would you describe your work style?
8. Tell me about yourself.
9. Are you willing to relocate?
10. Why do you think we should hire you for this job?
11. How do you define success?
12. What area of this job would you find most difficult?

13. What is your greatest weakness?
14. What is your greatest strength?
15. What is the name of the last book you read?
16. What has been your greatest work crisis, and how did you solve it?
17. Why did you choose this particular field of work?
18. What do you see yourself doing in 5 or 10 years?
19. What are your salary requirements?
20. How do you work under pressure?
21. Describe a conflict you've had with a coworker. How did you resolve it?
22. What school courses did you like best and least?
23. How soon can you start work?

The On-Site Interview

If you've had multiple on-site interviews and have yet to find a match, your interviewing skills might need some adjustment. While mastering the interviewing process is challenging, practice and preparation will put you in a good position to land the job.

Before the Interview

Actors don't take the stage without first dressing for their parts and rehearsing their lines. Likewise, you wouldn't want to go into an interview unprepared.

❏ *Know yourself, the company, and the position.* Compile a portfolio of your work accomplishments, and focus on skills that apply to the open position. Read the corporate Web site to get a feel for the company's environment, products and services, financial trends, and major achievements. Memorize the job description, including responsibilities and required skills.

❏ *Plan your answers.* Practice your answers to common interview questions. Be sure to turn negatives into positives. *("Perfectionism is a weakness of mine, but it certainly helps when thousands of people are relying on my systems.")*

❏ *Plan your attire.* Dress for success, even if the company has a casual dress code. One word, *conservative*, summarizes how you should dress for an interview. Everything about you should be clean and neat, including your hair, teeth, hands, fingernails, and clothes.

❏ *Give yourself plenty of time.* Don't schedule two interviews on the same day unless you are absolutely certain that you can be on time for the second interview without having to leave the first one early. Ask approximately how long the interview will take and how many people you will be meeting. Give yourself extra time for the commute.

- *Gather your papers.* Collect a portfolio of essential items to bring, including your resume and cover letter (the ones you used when applying for the position), letters of recommendation, references, and work samples. You may also need a work permit, driver's license, or social security card, and school transcripts if you're a recent graduate.

- *Prepare questions for the interviewer.* It's important to ask the interviewer questions about the position and the company, such as, *"What will my typical day be like?," "Why is this position available?,"* and *"In a perfect world, who would be the perfect candidate for this position and why?"* Asking questions shows that you know what you want, reveals things about the job that you might not have known, and can be useful when you need a few seconds to regroup.

- *Go to bed early.* Get plenty of sleep the night before, eat a decent breakfast that morning, and arrive well rested and alert. A blurry-eyed, blurry-minded interviewee will not impress a potential employer.

During the Interview

From the moment you enter a prospective employer's building until you say your good-byes, you're on stage. Follow this advice to ensure you make the most of every minute.

- *Make a strong first impression.* Your first impression is the most important moment of your interview. In the time it takes you to walk across the room, greet the interviewer, and sit down, he or she has already formed a strong opinion about you. Stand up straight and walk with confidence. Introduce yourself, smile, and shake hands firmly.

- *Maintain a positive attitude.* Be polite and gracious throughout your interview. Show that you are genuinely interested in the job, and project an air of optimism and goodwill.

- *Watch your language.* Speak in standard English, use a clear, confident tone of voice, and avoid slang expressions. Listen attentively, and respond fully to questions. Watch your body language as well: Maintain eye contact, don't slouch, and don't fidget!

- *Emphasize your strengths.* Don't give employers the opportunity to dwell on your weaknesses. Even if the interviewer seems interested in the ugly truth about your cruel previous employer, maintain your professionalism. Never, *ever* speak poorly of a former employer, regardless of how true it might be! Don't focus on skills you don't have. For example, instead of saying, *"I've never supervised other people before,"* say *"My work teams often mention my strong leadership skills, and I'm confident I'll be a good supervisor."*

❏ ***Thank the interviewer.*** When the interview is finished, shake hands firmly and thank the interviewer by name. Restate your interest in the position, and inquire about the next step in the interview process. If you haven't already been given a business card, ask for one.

5 STAR WEB SITES

Need pointers for writing a post-interview thank-you letter? Monster's online career center offers helpful suggestions and free letter samples. Check it out at **http://content.monster.com/ resume/samples/thankyou**

After the Interview

Your work isn't finished just because the interview is over. Your chances of winning a job improve significantly when you send a follow-up thank-you letter. Every interview is a learning experience. Your interviewing skills will improve considerably if you take the time to review and evaluate your meeting.

❏ ***Thank the interviewer.*** Send the interviewer a thank-you letter immediately following your interview—no later than one day after your meeting. Reaffirm your interest in the position, restate your qualifications for the position, and express appreciation for the interviewer's time and courtesy. A brief, well-written note may swing the balance in your favor when the employer makes the final decision.

❏ ***Evaluate your performance.*** While the interview is still fresh in your mind, review it and assess your effectiveness. Think about what you did well and how you can improve. Record your assessment and study it before your next interview.

 Checkpoint

1. Describe three ways to create an effective telephone interview environment.

_____

_____

_____

2. Give an example of turning a negative question into a positive statement about your abilities.

_____

_____

It's a Wrap

❏ If you're not getting the responses you hoped for from your job search, you may need to monitor and refine your Internet job search based on your results. Strategies for increasing your success include using resume views, keywords, and resume and job board services.

❏ If your Internet job search has generated plenty of views, detailed views, and calls from employers and you're still not getting on-site interviews, you might need to improve your telephone and e-mail communication with recruiters during the pre-interview screening.

❏ If you've had multiple on-site interviews and have yet to find a match, your interviewing skills might need some adjustment. While mastering the interviewing process is challenging, practice and preparation will put you in a good position to land the job.

Learn the Lingo

Match each term to its definition.

Terms
___ **1.** detailed view
___ **2.** emoticon
___ **3.** resume "blasting"
___ **4.** view

Definitions

a. an acronym for *emotion icon;* a small icon composed of punctuation characters that indicates the sender's emotion

b. when a recruiter reviews your complete resume

c. when your resume summary appears in a recruiter's search results

d. using a fee-based service to send your resume via fax or e-mail to thousands of companies and/or third-party recruiters

E-valuation

1. Using the strategies provided in this chapter, diagnose your greatest job-seeking weakness. For example, if your greatest weakness is interviewing, identify your specific problems. Create a detailed, step-by-step plan for overcoming the problems, and work on fixing them.

2. Get together with one or two peers who are currently looking for work. Video tape each other performing mock interviews. Using common interview questions, take turns playing the roles of interviewer and interviewee. Provide feedback for each interviewee.

WEB SITE DIRECTORY

THE CREAM OF THE CROP

Visit
JobSeekerSecrets.com
for a larger, consistently-updated version of this job board directory.

6FigureJobs.com™ (www.6figurejobs.com)

6FigureJobs.com™ should be a staple site for executive-level job seekers. This site is one of the best for senior sales positions.

America's Job Bank (www.jobsearch.org)

America's Job Bank is provided by the U.S. Department of Labor and various state employment offices. Search both the general database and the state-specific databases. This site allows users to search by military specialty codes, a capability not found on most job boards.

CareerBuilder® (www.careerbuilder.com)

CareerBuilder® is partnered with a number of newspapers across the country and therefore lists jobs that may not be found on other general job boards. With its user-friendly interface, this site is an essential destination for your job search.

CareerJournal.com (www.careerjournal.com)

CareerJournal.com, *The Wall Street Journal's* career site, offers reprints of newspaper postings as well as online-only postings. Executive-level job seekers will find a variety of quality career articles and features.

ComputerJobs.com® (www.computerjobs.com)

This top-four IT job board offers both national and local listings. ComputerJobs.com® is a valuable resource for the tech-minded job seeker.

Dice™ (www.dice.com)

Dice™ is the original technology job board and a consistent favorite of IT professionals. This site also lists a wide range of technical sales positions.

Experience™ (www.experience.com)

Experience™ is the leading provider of career networks for colleges, universities, and employers seeking to hire educated talent.

FlipDog.com™ (www.flipdog.com)

This site's job listings are all directly from the source: company Web sites. FlipDog.com™ searches the Web to bring you the Internet's largest job collection.

HotJobs® (www.hotjobs.com)

Packed with listings and career advice, HotJobs® is another must for your job search. Unlike most job boards, this site allows users to view job listings from only direct employers, only staffing firms, or both.

JobSeekerSecrets.com (www.jobseekersecrets.com)
JobSeekerSecrets.com is the online destination for this book. Besides providing an online version of the book, the site provides updates, best-of-breed career resources, screened and rated job seeker services, and member discounts.

Monster® (www.monster.com)
The largest job board in the business (with almost four times more traffic than its nearest competitor), Monster® offers a wealth of information, career content, and career resources. This site is a staple for most employers and a must for your job search.

Net-Temps (www.net-temps.com)
This site is a great resource for temporary and full-time job opportunities. Net-Temps is a long-term player that has grown consistently through the years.

The New York Times on the Web (www.nytimes.com)
The New York Times' job board is a tremendous resource for job seekers in the tristate area of New York, New Jersey, and Connecticut. This site also offers a wealth of career-related content written by some of the best writers in the business.

The Riley Guide (www.rileyguide.com)
The Riley Guide has been named "Best Job-Hunt Tutorial" by *Yahoo! Internet Life* for three years running. Margaret Riley Dikel provides tons of information about a variety of job-search-related subjects.

Spherion® Interim Executives (www.imcor.com)
Spherion® Interim Executives is a leading provider of temporary executives. Visit the site if you are open to short-term executive positions.

Techies.com® (www.techies.com)
With its strong history as a technical career site and its diverse list of job openings, Techies.com® should be on every IT professional's must-visit list.

Top Echelon® Network, Inc. (www.topechelon.com)
The Top Echelon® Network consists of thousands of recruiters who post their open positions to the Web site. The site allows users to search a recruiter database for contact information.

Vault℠ (www.vaultreports.com)
Vault℠ made a name for itself by providing in-depth company profiles, including The Electronic Watercooler™, which provides inside information about what it's *really* like to work for companies.

JOB BOARDS AND CAREER SITES

The 4Business Network℠: **www.4jobs.com**

4Work.com: **www.4work.com**

Americahasjobs.com℠: **www.americahasjobs.com**

AmericanJobs.com®: **www.americanjobs.com**

AreaJobs.com: **www.areajobs.com**

BestJobsUSA.com: **www.bestjobsusa.com**

BrassRing™: **www.1-jobs.com**

Career.com™: **www.career.com**

Careerbuzz: **www.careerbuzz.com**

CareerCity®: **www.careercity.com**

CareerExchange: **www.careerexchange.com**

Careernet: **www.careernet.com**

CareerShop: **www.careershop.com**

CoolWorks®: **www.coolworks.com**

DirectEmployers: **www.directemployers.com**

DirectJobs: **www.directjobs.com**

Ejobstores.com: **www.ejobstores.com**

EmployMAX: **www.employmax.com**

Employment.com®: **www.employment.com**

EmploymentGuide.com: **www.careerweb.com**

Employment Wizard: **www.employmentwizard.com**

EmployOn℠: **www.employon.com**

GrassIsGreener®: **www.grassisgreener.com**

Job.com: **www.job.com**

Jobfind.com: **www.jobfind.com**

JobOpps.net: **www.jobopps.net**

JobOptions™: **www.joboptions.com**

Jobshark: **www.jobshark.com**

Jobsinthemoney: **www.jobsinthemoney.com**

JobsOnline™: **www.jobsonline.com**

Jobsquare: **www.jobsquare.com**

Mycareer.com: **www.mycareer.com**

NationJob Network™: **www.nationsjobs.com**

ProfessionalJobNetwork.com: **www.nationaljobnetwork.com**

Thingamajob℠: **www.thingamajob.com**

TrueCareers℠: **www.truecareers.com**

USA Today® Careers Network: **http://careers.usatoday.com**

US Careers Resource Center℠: **www.uscareers.com**

USJobs.com: **www.usjobs.com**

The Wall Street Journal Online: **www.wsj.com**

Wanted Jobs: **www.wantedjobs.com**

WorkLife™: **www.worklife.com**

Yahoo!® Careers: **http://careers.yahoo.com**

REGIONAL SITES

Alabama

Al.com Careers: **www.al.com/careers**

Alabama's Job Bank: **www.ajb.org/al**

Alabama Works: **www.alabamaworks.org**

The Dothan Eagle: **www.dothaneagle.com**

EpriseNow Village: **www.eprisenow.com**

TimesDaily.com: **www.timesdaily.com**

Alaska

AkLA Jobs: **www.akla.org/jobs.htm**

Alaska Fishing Jobs Clearinghouse: **www.fishingjobs.com**

Alaska Job Center Network: **www.jobs.state.ak.us**

Alaska Jobs Center: **www.ilovealaska.com/alaskajobs**

Alaska's Job Bank:
www.labor.state.ak.us/esjobs/jobs

Alaska's World.com: **www.alaskasworld.com**

Anchorage Daily News: **www.adn.com**

Fairbanks Daily News-Miner:
www.news-miner.com

The Juneau Empire Online:
www.juneauempire.com

State of Alaska Jobs:
www.state.ak.us/local/jobs.html

Arizona

Arizona's Job Bank: **www.ajb.org/az**

ArizonaJobs.com: **www.arizonacareers.com**

Arizonahasjobs.com:
www.arizonahasjobs.com

Azcentral.com: **www.azcentral.com**

Big Deal Classifieds™ Online:
www.bigdealclassifieds.com

PhoenixEmployment.com:
www.phoenixemployment.com

PhoenixJobs.com: **www.phoenixjobs.com**

Arkansas

AccessArkansas.org Business & Employment:
www.state.ar.us/business.html

ArkansasBusiness.com:
www.arkansasbusiness.com

Arkansas Career Development Network:
www.accessarkansas.org/onestop/

Arkansas Employment Register:
www.arjobs.com

Arkansas Government Jobs:
www.arstatejobs.com

Arkansas' Job Bank: **www.ajb.org/ar**

ArkansasJobs.com: **www.arkansasjobs.com**

Arkansas Online®: **www.ardemgaz.com**

Arkansas STC Job Page:
www.stc-arkansas.org/jobs

Arkol.com: **www.arkol.com**

The Benton Courier: **www.bentoncourier.com**

GoArkansas.com: **www.goarkansas.com**

Greater Jonesboro Chamber of Commerce Job
Search: **www.jonesborojobs.org**

NWAonline.net: **www.nwaonline.net**

Whatajob.com: **www.whatajob.com**

California

BayArea.com: **www.bayarea.com**

CaliforniaJobs.com: **www.californiajobs.com**

The California Online Job Network:
www.cajobs.com

California State Personnel Board:
www.spb.ca.gov

California's Job Bank: **www.ajb.org/ca**

CalJobs^{SM}: **www.caljobs.ca.gov**

Craigslist®: **www.craigslist.com**

InsideBayArea.com: **www.insidebayarea.com**

JobStar: **http://jobstar.org**

Los Angeles Times: **www.latimes.com**

MontereyHerald.com: **www.montereyca.com**

NewsChoice:
www.newschoice.com/default.asp

Palo Alto Online: **www.paloaltoonline.com**

The Sacramento Bee: **www.sacbee.com**

SFGate.com: **www.sfgate.com**

Tri-City Weekly: **www.tricityweekly.com**

Colorado

Boulder Community Network:
http://bcn.boulder.co.us

Colorado's Job Bank: **www.ajb.org/co**

DenverPost.com: **www.denverpost.com**

Employment Wizard:
www.employmentwizard.com

Rocky Mountain Jobs:
www.rockymountainjobs.com

Connecticut

The Advocate: **www.stamfordadvocate.com**

Connecticut's Job Bank: **www.ajb.org/ct**

Greenwich Time: **www.greenwichtime.com**

The Hartford Courant: **www.ctnow.com**

Delaware

DelawareOnline.com:
www.delawareonline.com

Delaware's Job Bank: **www.ajb.org/de**

Virtual Career Network: **www.vcnet.net**

District of Columbia

District of Columbia: City Government:
http://dc.gov/gov

District of Columbia's Job Bank:
www.ajb.org/dc

The Washington Post:
www.washingtonpost.com

Florida

FloridaCareerLINK:
www.floridacareerlink.com

Florida's Job Bank: **www.ajb.org/fl**

Miami.com: **www.miami.com**

MyFlorida.com™ Employment:
www2.myflorida.com

OrlandoJobs.com: **www.orlandojobs.com**

Orlando Sentinel: **www.orlandosentinel.com**

South Florida Sun-Sentinel:
www.sun-sentinel.com

Tallahassee.com: **www.tallahassee.com**

Georgia

AccessAtlanta.com®: **www.accessatlanta.com**

The Atlanta Journal-Constitution:
www.ajc.com

GeorgiaCareers.com:
www.georgiacareers.com

Georgiahasjobs.com℠:
www.georgiahasjobs.com

Georgia One-Stop Career Network:
www.g1careernet.com

Georgia's Job Bank: **www.ajb.org/ga**

Macon.com: **www.macon.com**

Hawaii

Hawaii.com: **www.hawaii.com**

Hawaii Department of Labor and Industrial
Relations: **http://dlir.state.hi.us**

Hawaii's Job Bank: **www.ajb.org/hi**

Idaho

Idaho's Job Bank: **www.ajb.org/id**

IdahoWorks℠: **www.idahoworks.state.id.us**

Illinois

Belleville.com: **www.belleville.com**

ChicagoJobs.com: **www.chicagojobs.com**

ChicagoJobs.org: **www.chicagojobs.org**

Chicago Tribune: **www.chicagotribune.com**

City of Chicago: **www.cityofchicago.org**

Illinois' Job Bank: **www.ajb.org/il**

The State Journal-Register Online:
www.sj-r.com

Chicago Sun-Times: **www.suntimes.com**

Indiana

HoosierNet: **www.bloomington.in.us**

Indianapolis OnLine: **www.indianapolis.in.us**

The Indianapolis Star: **www.starnews.com**

Indiana's Job Bank: **www.ajb.org/in**

Iowa

Iowa's Job Bank: **www.ajb.org/ia**

Iowa Workforce Development:
www.iowaworkforce.org

Kansas

AccessKansas: **www.accesskansas.org**

Kansas.com: **www.kansas.com**

KansasCity.com: **www.kansascity.com**

Kansas' Job Bank: **www.ajb.org/ks**

KansasJobLink: **www.kansasjoblink.com**

The Topeka Capital-Journal:
www.cjonline.com

Wichita Area Chamber of Commerce:
www.wichitakansas.org

Kentucky

The Courier-Journal: **www.courierjournal.com**

Kentucky.com: **www.kentucky.com**

Kentucky Cabinet for Workforce Development:
www.kycwd.org

Kentucky's Job Bank: **www.ajb.org/ky**

Louisiana

The Advocate Online: **www.theadvocate.com**

LouisianaJobMarket: **www.lajobmarket.com**

Louisiana's Job Bank: **www.ajb.org/la**

Nola.com: **www.nola.com**

Maine

Maine CareerCenter:
www.mainecareercenter.com

Maine's Job Bank: **www.ajb.org/me**

MaineToday.com Careers:
www.careers.mainetoday.com

Maryland

The Baltimore Sun: **www.baltimoresun.com**

HometownAnnapolis.com:
www.hometownannapolis.com

Maryland's CareerNet:
http://careernet.state.md.us

Maryland's Job Bank: **www.ajb.org/md**

Massachusetts

Boston.com: **www.boston.com**

Boston Online: **www.boston-online.com**

BostonSearch.com^SM: **www.bostonsearch.com**

eWorcester.com: **www.eworcester.com**

Massachusetts' Job Bank: **www.ajb.org/ma**

Town Online: **www.townonline.com**

Michigan

Michigan Department of Career Development:
www.michigan.gov/mdcd

Michigan Talent Bank: **www.michworks.org**

Minnesota

DuluthSuperior.com:
www.duluthsuperior.com

MinnesotaJobs.com: **www.minnesotajobs.com**

Minnesota WorkForce Center:
www.mnworkforcecenter.org

Minnesota's Job Bank: **www.ajb.org/mn**

Star Tribune: **www.startribune.com**

TwinCities.com: **www.twincities.com**

Mississippi

Mississippi.gov: **www.ms.gov**

Mississippi's Job Bank: **www.ajb.org/ms**

SunHerald.com: **www.mississippicoast.com**

Missouri

City of Kansas City, Missouri: **www.kcmo.org**

KansasCity.com: **www.kansascity.com**

Missouri's Job Bank: **www.ajb.org/mo**

Missouri WORKS!: **http://works.state.mo.us**

StLouisAtWork.com: **www.stlouisatwork.com**

STLtoday.com: **www.stltoday.com**

Montana

Billings Gazette: **www.billingsgazette.com**

DiscoveringMontana: **www.discoveringmontana.com**

Montana's Job Bank: **www.ajb.org/mt**

Nebraska

Careerlink.org®: **www.careerlink.org**

Lincolnjobs.com: **www.lincolnjobs.com**

Lincoln Journal Star: **www.journalstar.com**

Nebraska's Job Bank: **www.ajb.org/ne**

Omaha.com®: **www.omaha.com**

State of Nebraska: **www.nol.org**

Nevada

Lasvegas.com: **www.lasvegas.com**

Las Vegas Review-Journal: **www.lvrj.com**

NevadaNet: **www.nevadanet.com**

Nevada's Job Bank: **www.ajb.org/nv**

New Hampshire

New Hampshire Employment Security: **http://nhworks.state.nh.us**

NH.com: **www.nh.com**

The Telegraph Online: **www.nashuatelegraph.com**

New Jersey

INjersey.com: **www.injersey.com**

NewJersey.com: **www.newjersey.com**

New Jersey's Job Bank: **www.ajb.org/nj**

NJ Jobs: **www.njjobs.com**

NJ.com: **www.nj.com**

Philly.com: **www.philly.com**

New Mexico

The Albuquerque Journal Online: **www.abqjournal.com**

New Mexico's Job Bank: **www.ajb.org/nm**

New York

CareerZone®: **www.nycareerzone.org**

daVinci Jobs: **www.davincitimes.org**

Newsday.com: **www.newsday.com**

New York's Job Bank: **www.ajb.org/ny**

NYCareers.com: **www.nycareers.com**

Rochester Democrat and Chronicle: **www.democratandchronicle.com**

Syracuse.com: **www.syracuse.com**

WNYjobs.com: **www.wnyjobs.com**

North Carolina

CarolinasCareerWeb: **www.carolinascareerweb.com**

Charlotte.com: **www.charlotte.com**

CharlotteJobs.com: **www.charlottejobs.com**

Jobs.triangle.com: **www.triangle.com/jobs**

The Nando Times: **www.nando.net**

North Carolina's Job Bank: **www.ajb.org/nc**

RaleighJobs.com: **www.raleighjobs.com**

North Dakota

CareerLinkNorth.com: **www.careerlinknorth.com**

GrandForks.com: **www.grandforks.com**

JobsND.com: **state.nd.us/jsnd**

North Dakota's Job Bank: **www.ajb.org/nd**

Ohio

CareerBoard.com: **www.careerboard.com**

Cincinnati.com™: **www.cincinnati.com**

The Columbus Dispatch: **www.dispatch.com**

Monster® JobMatch Tristate: **www.jobmatch.com**

Ohio.com: **www.ohio.com**

Ohio JobNet On-Line: **www.state.oh.us/odjfs/ojn**

Ohio's Job Bank: **www.ajb.org/oh**

Oklahoma

NewsOK.com: **www.newsok.com**

Oklahoma Employment Security Commission: **www.oesc.state.ok.us**

Oklahoma's Job Bank: **www.ajb.org/ok**

Oregon

Mail Tribune: **www.mailtribune.com**

OregonLive.com: **www.oregonlive.com**

Portland Chamber Employment: **www.portlandchamber.com/jobbank**

Pennsylvania

Jobnet.com: **www.jobnet.com**

PA-Today: **www.pa-today.com**

Pennsylvania's Job Bank: **www.ajb.org/pa**

PhillyBurbs.com: **www.phillyburbs.com**

PhillyJobs.com: **www.phillyjobs.com**

PhillyWorks: **www.phillyworks.com**

PittsburghJobs.com: **www.pittsburghjobs.com**

Team Pennsylvania Foundation: **www.teampa.com**

TimesLeader.com: **www.timesleader.com**

Rhode Island

Projo.com: **www.projo.com**

Rhode Island's Job Bank: **www.ajb.org/ri**

South Carolina

CarolinasCareerWeb: **www.carolinascareerweb.com**

Charleston.Net: **www.charleston.net**

MyrtleBeachOnline.com: **www.myrtlebeachonline.com**

SCIway^{SM}: **www.sciway.net**

Southcarolinahasjobs.com: **www.southcarolinahasjobs.com**

South Carolina's Job Bank: **www.ajb.org/sc**

South Dakota

AberdeenNews.com: **www.aberdeennews.com**

Argus Leader: **www.argusleader.com**

Rapid City Journal: **www.rapidcityjournal.com**

SiouxFalls.com: **www.siouxfalls.com**

South Dakota's Job Bank: **www.ajb.org/sd**

Tennessee

GoMemphis.com: **www.gomemphis.com**

KnoxCareers.com: **www.knoxcareers.com**

The Knoxville News-Sentinel: **www.knoxnews.com**

Nashville JobsLink: **www.nashvillejobslink.com**

The Tennessean: **www.tennessean.com**

Tennessee's Job Bank: **www.ajb.org/tn**

Texas

Austin360.com^{SM}: **www.austin360.com**

AustinEmployment.com: **www.austinemployment.com**

AustinJobs.com: **www.austinjobs.com**

The Dallas Morning News: **www.dallasnews.com**

DFW.com: **www.dfw.com**

DFWEmployment.com: **www.dfwemployment.com**

Galveston County Daily News: **www.galvnews.com**

HoustonEmployment.com: **www.houstonemployment.com**

HoustonChronicle.com: **www.chron.com**

HoustonJobs.com: **www.houstonjobs.com**

MySA.com: **www.mysanantonio.com**

Texas' Job Bank: **www.ajb.org/tx**

TexasJobs.com: **www.texasjobs.com**

Utah

The Deseret News: **www.deseretnews.com**

HarkTheHerald.com: **www.harktheherald.com**

Utah's Job Bank: **www.ajb.org/ut**

Vermont

The Addison County Independent: **www.addisonindependent.com**

Vermont's Job Bank: **www.ajb.org/vt**

Virginia

CareerConnect©: **www.careerconnect.state.va.us**

The Daily Press: **www.dailypress.com**

HamptonRoads.com: **www.hamptonroads.com**

Richmond Times-Dispatch: **www.timesdispatch.com**

Virginia's Job Bank: **www.ajb.org/va**

Washington

SeattleJobs.com: **www.seattlejobs.com**

The Seattle Times: **www.seattletimes.com**

Spokane.net™: **www.spokane.net**

Spokanehasjobs.com℠: **www.spokanehasjobs.com**

Washington's Job Bank: **www.ajb.org/wa**

West Virginia

The Charleston Gazette Online: **www.wvgazette.com**

The Dominion Post: **www.dominionpost.com**

West Virginia's Job Bank: **www.ajb.org/wv**

Wisconsin

Madison.com: **www.madison.com**

Milwaukee Journal Sentinel: **www.jsonline.com**

Wisconsin's Job Bank: **www.ajb.org/wi**

Wyoming

Wyoming Department of Employment: **http://wydoe.state.wy.us**

Wyoming Job Network: **http://onestop.state.wy.us**

Wyoming's Job Bank: **www.ajb.org/wy**

Canada

CanadaIT.com: **www.canadait.com**

CanadaJobs.com: **www.canadajobs.com**

HotJobs.ca™: **www.hotjobs.ca**

Jobboom.com: **www.jobboom.com**

Job Bus Canada: **www.jobbus.com**

Midlyn.com: **www.canadacareers.com**

Monster.ca: **www.monster.ca**

SPECIALTY SITES

Advancing Women™: **www.advancingwomen.com**

American Society of Women Accountants: **www.aswa.org**

Asian American Economic Development Enterprises: **www.aaede.org**

Asian American Journalists Assoc.: **www.aaja.org**

Association for Women in Communications: **www.womcom.org**

Assoc. of Latino Professionals in Finance and Accounting: **www.alpfa.org**

Assoc. for Women in Science: **www.awis.org**

BestDiversityEmployers.com: **www.bestdiversityemployers.com**

Bilingual-Jobs: **www.bilingual-jobs.com**

Black Career Women: **www.bcw.org**

The Black Collegian Online: **www.black-collegian.com**

Blackenterprise.com: **www.blackenterprise.com**

The Black E.O.E. Journal: **www.blackeoejournal.com**

BlackVoices.com: **www.blackvoices.com**

The Black World Today: **www.blackworldtoday.com**

Corporate Diversity Search: **www.corpdiversitysearch.com**

CVlatino.com^{SM}: **www.cvlatino.com**

DisabilityDirect.gov: **www.disabilitydirect.gov**

DiversiLink: **www.diversilink.com**

Diversity.com: **www.diversity.com**

Diversity Employment: **www.diversityemployment.com**

Diversityforhire.com: **www.diversityforhire.com**

DiversityInc.com: **www.diversityinc.com**

DiversityJobLink.com: **www.diversityjoblink.com**

Diversity Job Network™: **www.diversityjobnetwork.com**

DiversityRecruiting.com: **www.diversityrecruiting.com**

DiversitySearch: **www.diversitysearch.com**

eFAAB™: **www.efaab.net**

Employers EEO Journal: **www.employers-eeo-journal.com**

Equal Opportunity Publications: **www.eop.com**

Financial Women International: **www.fwi.org**

HireDiversity.com: **www.hirediversity.com**

HispanicOnline.com: **www.hispaniconline.com**

Idealist: **www.idealist.org**

iHispano.com: **www.ihispano.com**

The Immigration Portal: **www.ilw.com**

IMdiversity.com: **www.imdiversity.com**

iMinorities.com: **www.iminorities.com**

iVillage™ Work Channel: **www.ivillage.com/work**

Job Accommodation Network: **www.jan.wvu.edu**

JobAccess: **www.jobaccess.org**

JobCentro.com: **www.jobcentro.com**

Jobs4Women.com: **www.jobs4women.com**

JobSquare: **www.jobsquare.com**

LatPro.com: **www.latpro.com**

MinorityCareer.com: **www.minoritycareer.com**

MinorityGraduate.com: **www.minoritygraduate.com**

MinorityNurse.com: **www.minoritynurse.com**

National Assoc. of Black Accountants: **http://nabainc.jobcontrolcenter.com**

National Assoc. of Black Journalists Online: **www.nabj.org**

National Business and Disability Council: **www.business-disability.com**

The National Diversity Newspaper Job Bank: **www.newsjobs.com**

National Society of Black Engineers: **www.nsbe.org**

National Society of Hispanic MBAs: **www.nshmba.org**

Network of Commercial Real Estate Women: **www.crewnetwork.org**

RecruitABILITY™: **www.recruit-ability.com**

Saludos.com: **www.saludos.com**

Society of Women Engineers: **www.swe.org**

Teens4hire®: **www.teens4hire.com**

WorkplaceDiversity: **www.workplacediversity.com**

INDUSTRY SITES

Administrative and Telemarketing Jobs

All Bookkeeping Resource:
www.allbookkeepingresource.com

BookkeeperJobs.com:
www.bookkeeperjobs.com

CallCenterCareers.com:
www.callcentercareers.com

CallCenterJobs.com: **www.callcenterjobs.com**

CallCenterOps: **www.callcenterops.com**

Call Center Times: **www.callcentertimes.com**

iHireSecretarial: **www.ihiresecretarial.com**

Receptionistjobstore.com:
www.receptionistjobstore.com

VirtualAssistants.com:
www.virtualassistants.com

Education and Child Care Jobs

4nannies.com: **www.4nannies.com**

Child Care Career Centre:
www.childcare.net/careers.shtml

K-12jobs.com: **http://k12jobs.com**

Nannyjob: **www.nannyjob.co.uk**

National Teacher Recruitment Clearinghouse:
www.recruitingteachers.org

Teachers@Work: **www.teachersatwork.com**

Teach for America: **www.teachforamerica.org**

TeachingJobs.com: **www.teachingjobs.com**

Engineering and Industrial Jobs

Aerospace Online^{SM}:
www.aerospaceonline.com

AMTonline.com: **www.amtonline.com**

Auto Central^{SM}: **www.autocentral.com**

Aviation Jobs Online^{TM}:
www.aviationjobsonline.com

Careers in Construction:
www.careersinconstruction.com

ConstructionJobs.com^{SM}:
www.constructionjobs.com

Constructionmanagerjob.com:
www.constructionmanagerjob.com

ConstructionWork.com$^{®}$:
www.constructionwork.com

Digital Broadcasting^{SM}:
www.digitalbroadcasting.com

Electricianjobs.com: **www.electricianjobs.com**

ElectronicsWeb^{SM}: **www.electronicsweb.com**

Engineeremployment.com:
www.engineeremployment.com

EngineeringCentral.com^{TM}:
www.engineeringcentral.com

EngineerJobs.com: **www.engineerjobs.com**

Facilitymanagerjobs.com:
www.facilitymanagerjobs.com

HVAC Agent: **www.hvacagent.com**

iHireBuildingTrades:
www.ihirebuildingtrades.com

Institute of Electrical and Electronics
Engineers: **www.ieee.org**

MaterialsJobs.com: **www.materialsjobs.com**

MECHdata, Inc.: **www.mechdata.com**

Photonics Online^{SM}:
www.photonicsonline.com

PhotonicsJobs.com: **www.photonicsjobs.com**

RF Globalnet^{SM}: **www.rfglobalnet.com**

Society of Automotive Engineers: **www.sae.org**

Society of Plastics Engineers: **www.4spe.org**

Trade Jobs Online: **www.tradejobsonline.com**

Welding.com: **www.welding.com**

WeldingJobs.com: **www.weldingjobs.com**

Finance and Accounting Jobs

Accountantjobs.com:
www.accountantjobs.com

AccountantsWorld.com Jobs:
www.accountantsworld.com/jobs/

Accountemps®: **www.accountemps.com**

Accounting.com: **www.accounting.com**

AccountingClassifieds.com:
www.accountingclassifieds.com

AccountingJobsOnline.com:
www.accountingjobsonline.com

AccountingProfessional.com™:
www.accountingprofessional.com

American Accounting Assoc.: **www.aaahq.org**

American Assoc. of Finance and Accounting:
www.aafa.com

American Institute of CPAs: **www.aicpa.org**

AOC (Accountants on Call): **www.aocnet.com**

Assoc. for Financial Professionals:
www.afponline.org

Auditorjobs.com: **www.auditorjobs.com**

AwesomeAccountants.com:
www.awesomeaccountants.com

BetterManagement.com®:
www.bettermanagement.com

Big 5 Friends.com: **www.big5friends.com**

BigFiveTalent: **www.bigfivetalent.com**

Bloomberg.com: **www.bloomberg.com**

BookkeeperJobs.com:
www.bookkeeperjobs.com

BusinessAnalyst.com™:
www.businessanalyst.com

BusinessFinanceMag.com:
www.businessfinancemag.com

CareerBank.com: **www.careerbank.com**

CFO.com: **www.cfo.com**

CPAjobs.com: **www.cpajobs.com**

CreditJobsToday.com:
www.creditjobstoday.com

Doublecuff.com: **www.doublecuff.com**

D.W. Simpson & Company Actuarial Search:
www.actuaryjobs.com

eFinancialCareers:
www.efinancialcareers.com

ET Search, Inc.: **www.etsearch.com**

exBigFive.com: **www.exbigfive.com**

Financejobstore: **www.financejobstore.com**

Financial Job Network:
www.financialjobnetwork.com

FinancialJobs.com: **www.financialjobs.com**

FinancialPositions.com:
www.financialpositions.com

Financial Women International: **www.fwi.org**

Fincareer: **www.fincareer.com**

GAAPweb: **www.gaapweb.com**

iHireAccounting: **www.ihireaccounting.com**

The Institute of Internal Auditors:
www.theiia.org

Investmentbankingjobs.com:
www.investmentbankingjobs.com

JobServe Accountancy:
www.accountancy.jobserve.com

Jobsinthemoney: **www.jobsinthemoney.com**

Kutcher Tax Careers: **www.taxcareers.com**

LenderCareers℠: **www.lendercareers.com**

LocalAccountingJobs.com:
www.localaccountingjobs.com

MoneyCareers.com™:
www.moneycareers.com

SmartPros Accounting:
http://accounting.pro2net.com

Tax-Jobs.com: **www.tax-jobs.com**

Hospitality Jobs

E-Hospitality℠: **www.e-hospitality.com**

Hcareers.com: **www.hcareers.com**

Hospitalitycareernet.com:
www.hospitalitycareernet.com

HospitalityJobsOnline:
www.hospitalityonline.com

Hospitality Jobs Online℠: **www.hjo.net**

Human Resources Jobs

AIRS Recruiter Jobs:
www.airsrecruiterjobs.com

BenefitNews.com: **www.benefitnews.com**

CareersinRecruitment:
www.careersinrecruitment.com

College & University Professional Assoc. for Human Resources: **www.cupa.org**

Electronic Recruiting Exchange:
www.erexchange.com

Empty.net: **www.empty.net**

HR.com™: **www.hr.com**

HR Additions: **www.hradditions.com**

HR Hub℠: **www.hrhub.com**

HR Job Net: **www.hrjobnet.com**

HRMJobs.com: **www.hrmjobs.com**

iHireHR: **www.ihirehr.com**

Jobs4HR: **www.jobs4hr.com**

JobsInRecruiting.com:
www.jobsinrecruiting.com

Northeast Human Resources Assoc.:
www.nehra.com

RecruiterSeek.com: **www.recruiterseek.com**

RecruitersForum.com:
www.recruitersforum.com

Recruitmentjobz.com:
www.recruitmentjobz.com

Society for Human Resource Management:
www.shrm.org/jobs

TrainerQuest.com: **www.trainerquest.com**

Information Technology Jobs

Brainbuzz.com℠: **www.brainbuzz.com**

CareerMarketplace.com IT Sites:
www.careermarketplace.com/it.htm

COBOLJobs.com: **www.coboljobs.com**

Computerwork.com™:
www.computerwork.com

C++ Jobs: **www.cplusplusjobs.com**

C++Search.com: **www.cplusplussearch.com**

DatabaseJobs.com: **www.databasejobs.com**

ITcareers.com: **www.itcareers.com**

ITClassifieds.com: **www.itclassifieds.com**

JavaSearch.com: **www.javasearch.com**

JobCircle™: **www.jobcircle.com**

JustTechJobs.com: **www.justtechjobs.com**

LANJobs.com: **www.lanjobs.com**

LotusNotesJobs.com: **www.lotusnotesjobs.com**

OperationIT: **www.operationit.com**

ORAsearch.com: **www.orasearch.com**

Tech-Engine: **www.techengine.com**

TechJobBank: **www.techjobbank.com**

TelecomWeb: **www.telecomweb.com**

US Internet Industry Assoc.: **www.usiia.org**

VBasicSearch.com: **www.vbasicsearch.com**

VisualBasicJobs.com:
www.visualbasicjobs.com

WebJobsUSA.com: **www.webjobsusa.com**

WebProgrammingJobs.com:
www.webprogrammingjobs.com

Media and Visual Arts Jobs

ArtJobOnline: **www.artjob.org**

CreativeCentral.com:
www.creativecentral.com

Ekdahl & Associates:
http://photoimagingjobs.com

EntertainmentCareers.net[SM]:
www.entertainmentcareers.com

Graphicdesignerjobs.com:
www.graphicdesignerjobs.com

OnAirJobs.com™: **www.onairjobs.com**

TVandRadioJobs.com:
http://tvandradiojobs.com

TVJobs.com: **www.tvjobs.com**

Medical and Healthcare Jobs

Allnurses.com: **www.allnurses.com**

Alternativehealthjobs.com:
www.alternativehealthjobs.com

American Academy of Physician Assistants:
www.aapa.org

American Assoc. of Homes and Services for
the Aging: **www.aahsa.org**

American Assoc. of Medical Assistants:
www.aama-ntl.org

American Assoc. of Oral and Maxillofacial
Surgeons: **www.aaoms.org**

American College of Cardiology: **www.acc.org**

American College of Chest Physicians:
www.chestnet.org

American Dietetic Assoc.: **www.eatright.org**

American Psychiatric Assoc.: **www.psych.org**

American Psychiatric Nurses Assoc.:
www.apna.org

American Society for Clinical Pathology:
www.ascp.org

American Society of General Surgeons:
www.theasgs.org

American Society of Radiologic Technologists:
www.asrt.org

America's Health Care Source:
www.healthcaresource.com

Assistedlivingjobs.com:
www.assistedlivingjobs.com

Bio.com: **www.bio.com**

BioSpace®: **www.biospace.com**

BioView.com: **www.bioview.com**

CompHealth®: **www.medimorphus.com**

DentalAssistantJobs.com:
www.dentalassistantjobs.com

Dentalink.net: **www.dentalink.net**

Dental Practice Assistant:
www.dental--assistant.com

HCRecruiters.com: **www.hcrecruiters.com**

HealthCare Hub: **www.healthcarehub.com**

Health Care Job Store:
www.healthcarejobstore.com

Health Care Jobs Online:
www.hcjobsonline.com

HealthcareMatch[SM]:
www.healthcarematch.com

Health Care Recruitment Online™:
www.healthcarerecruitment.com

HealthCareerWeb.com:
www.healthcareerweb.com

HMonster: **http://myh.monster.com**

HospitaljobsUSA.com:
www.hospitaljobsusa.com

Jobscience.com™: **www.jobscience.com**

LabJobsOnline.com: **www.labjobsonline.com**

Laboratoryjobs.com: **www.laboratoryjobs.com**

MDrecruitmentonline.com:
www.mdrecruitmentonline.com

MedCareers: **www.medcareers.com**

MedHunters.com: **www.medhunters.com**

Medical Group Management Assoc.:
www.mgma.org

Medical Search Online:
www.msoworldwide.com

MedicalWorkers.com:
www.medicalworkers.com

Medoptions.com: **www.medoptions.com**

MedScouts: **www.medscouts.com**

MomMD: **www.mommd.com**

NurseWeek.com: **www.nurseweek.com**

NursingCenter: **www.nursingcenter.com**

Nursing-Jobs.com: **www.nursing-jobs.com**

Nursing Spectrum®:
www.nursingspectrum.com

Paramedicjobs.com: **www.paramedicjobs.com**

PharmacyJobsOnline.com:
www.pharmacyjobsonline.com

PhysicianBoard: **www.physicianboard.com**

PhysicianJobs.com™: **www.physicianjobs.com**

RehabCareer.com: **www.rehabcareer.com**

RehabWorld.com: **www.rehabworld.com**

The *SciWeb* Biotechnology Career Center:
www.biocareer.com

Social Work and Social Services Jobs Online:
http://gwbweb.wustl.edu/jobs

TherapyJobs.com: **www.therapyjobs.com**

Travel Health Care Online™:
www.travelhealthcareonline.com

Military, Government, and Public Service Jobs

911hotjobs.com™: **www.911hotjobs.com**

Careers in Government:
www.careersingovernment.com

Corporate Gray Online:
www.greentogray.com

Federal Jobs Digest: **www.jobsfed.com**

GoArmy.com: **www.goarmy.com**

Govtjobs.com: **www.govtjobs.com**

LawEnforcementJobs.com:
www.lawenforcementjobs.com

Marines.com: **www.marines.com**

Navy.com: **www.navy.com**

Park Law Enforcement Assoc.:
www.parkranger.com

PoliceEmployment.com:
www.policeemployment.com

Public Service Employees Network:
www.pse-net.com

Today's Military: **www.todaysmilitary.com**

U.S. Air Force: **www.airforce.com**

USAJOBS: **www.usajobs.opm.gov**

Natural Resources and Agriculture Jobs

AG Careers: **www.agricareers.com**

AgJobsUSA: **www.agjobsusa.com**

Agriculture Jobs:
http://agriculture-jobs.411jobs.net

AgricultureJobSite.com:
www.agriculturejobsite.com

American Meat Science Assoc.:
www.meatscience.org

BlueSkySearch.com: **www.blueskysearch.com**

EnvironmentalCareer.com:
www.environmentalcareer.com

Environmental Career Opportunities:
www.ecojobs.com

HorticulturalJobs.com:
www.horticulturaljobs.com

JobMonkey.com Great Outdoors:
www.jobmonkey.com/parks

Jobs In Horticulture Inc.ᔆᴹ: **www.hortjobs.com**

Meat and Poultry Online ᔆᴹ:
www.meatandpoultryonline.com

PoultryJobs.com™: **www.poultryjobs.com**

Sales Jobs

AccountManager.com™:
www.accountmanager.com

ComputerJobs.com® Technical Sales: **www.technicalsales.computerjobs.com**

Internetsalesjobs.com: **www.internetsalesjobs.com**

Jobs4Sales.com: **www.jobs4sales.com**

Justsell.com™: **www.justsell.com**

JustTechSalesJobs.com: **www.justtechsalesjobs.com**

Medicalsalesjobs.com: **www.medicalsalesjobs.com**

SalesClassifieds.com: **www.salesclassifieds.com**

SalesEngineer.com™: **www.salesengineer.com**

SalesHeads.com℠: **www.salesheads.com**

SalesJobADay: **www.salesjobaday.com**

SalesJobs.com®: **www.salesjobs.com**

Salesjobstore.com: **www.salesjobstore.com**

SalesRecruits.com: **www.salesrecruits.com**

SalesTrax: **www.salestrax.com**

SalesVacancies.com: **www.salesvacancies.com**

SellingJobs.com: **www.sellingjobs.com**

TeleSalesPositions.com: **www.telesalespositions.com**

TopSalesPositions.com: **www.topsalespositions.com**

FREELANCING SITES

A2Zmoonlighter.com: **www.a2zmoonlighter.com**

All Freelance Work: **www.allfreelancework.com**

Brainbid.com™: **www.brainbid.com**

Consultants-on-Demand.com: **www.consultants-on-demand.com**

ContractJobHunter: **www.cjhunter.com**

Contract-Jobs.com: **www.contract-jobs.com**

Creative Freelancers: **www.freelancers.com**

Do A Project.com: **www.doaproject.com**

eClaro: **www.eclaro.com**

Elance™: **www.elance.com**

eWork®: **www.ework.com**

FreeAgent.com℠: **www.freeagent.com**

FreelanceJobSearch: **www.freelancejobsearch.com**

Freelance Online: **www.freelanceonline.com**

Freelance Writing: **www.freelancewriting.com**

Guru®: **www.guru.com**

HotDispatch™: **www.hotdispatch.com**

ITconsultantjobs.com: **www.itconsultantjobs.com**

MediaStreet.com: **www.mediastreet.com**

Mom's Work at Home Site: **www.momsworkathomesite.com**

MoneyfromHome.com: **www.moneyfromhome.com**

National Technical Employment Services: **www.ntes.com**

Onvia: **www.onvia.com**

Outsource2000™: **www.outsource2000.org**

PortaJobs: **www.portajobs.com**

ProSavvy™: **www.prosavvy.com**

Research Network: **www.researchnetwork.com**

Software Contractors' Guild℠: **www.scguild.com**

Sologig.com™: **www.sologig.com**

Subcontract.com: **www.subcontract.com**

SwiftWork.com: **www.swiftwork.com**

TalentGateway: **www.talentgateway.com**

A

Active job seeker someone who is not employed in his or her chosen career and needs or wants work in a short period of time (p. 9)

ASCII American Standard Code for Information Interchange; a simple form of text that most computers can read and process (p. 40)

Avocation an intense interest or activity outside the workplace (p. 137)

B

Bookmark to save the address of a favorite Web page in an electronic list for easy access (p. 81)

Boolean search a search that includes logical operators, such as *AND, OR,* and *NOT* (p. 49)

Browser a program, such as Microsoft Internet Explorer or Netscape Navigator, that enables users to receive and display Web pages (p. 14)

Built resume a resume that you build by inputting sections of your electronic plain-text resume into a wizard (p. 42)

Bulletin board system an electronic version of a community bulletin board that allows users to post discussions, information, and often job openings (p. 14)

C

Career site a Web site that offers advice about searching and applying for job openings (p. 35)

Career target list a prioritized list of careers that you might be suited for (p. 31)

Chronological resume a resume that arranges work experience according to time sequence (most recent first) (p. 46)

Compensation the total value of an employee's salary and benefits (p. 29)

Confidentiality control over a specific employer's access to your information (pp. 8, 93)

Consulting being paid to give expert advice on a particular subject (p. 150)

Contingency search firms third-party recruiters who are paid only when they fill a position (p. 114)

Contingent dependent on something that may or may not occur (p. 114)

Corporate site a Web site for a particular company; often, but not always, offers information about the company's job openings (p. 35)

Cover letter a letter that introduces a resume; sent when submitting a formal application for a job opening (p. 65)

Cross-posting the practice of sharing the same job listings on multiple job boards (p. 97)

D

Directory a database with Web site content descriptions that are developed by Web site owners or independent human reviewers (pp. 14, 73)

Detailed view when a recruiter reviews your complete resume (p. 163)

Display advertisements large advertisements with graphic elements that are separated from print-only advertisements (p. 125)

E

E-recruiting electronic recruiting; the practice of finding candidates for job openings through the Internet (p. 10)

Electronic resume a resume that is delivered electronically (p. 40)

Emoticon an acronym for *emotion icon;* a small icon composed of punctuation characters that indicates the sender's emotion (p. 171)

Employee referral systems programs that reward employees for referring candidates for open positions (p. 112)

F

FAQ (Frequently Asked Questions) questions and answers posted by most Web sites that can be used as tools for finding information, troubleshooting problems, and learning the rules and etiquette for a particular Web site (p. 14)

Freelancing working without committing to a particular employer (p. 149)

Functional resume a resume that focuses on skills, personal attributes, and any relevant volunteer or job experience (p. 46)

G

Government career site a Web site that lists job openings for various branches of government (p. 36)

Government employment agencies city and state organizations that provide general employment opportunities in a given area (p. 129)

H

Home page the first page that opens when you log on to the Internet or a Web site's opening page or main page (p. 14)

HTML abbreviation of hypertext markup language, the language used for creating Web sites (pp. 14, 63)

hyperlink a word, phrase, or Web site address that is set off with separate colors and underlining; clicking on a hyperlink sends you to another Web page (p. 15)

I

Identity thieves people who steal others' personal information to apply for credit or commit other crimes (p. 93)

Industry a specific field of employment (p. 20)

Industry association an organization of businesses, institutions, or other entities that promotes, and sometimes sets standards for, an industry (p. 135)

Industry site a Web site that offers career information and job openings for a specific field of employment (p. 36)

Internet job search a job search that primarily uses the Internet to find and respond to job listings (p. 2)

Internet Service Provider (ISP) a company that provides access to the Internet for a monthly fee; also referred to as access provider, service provider, and connectivity provider (p. 15)

Invoice a written record of goods or services provided and the amount charged for them that is sent to a customer as a request for payment (p. 155)

J

Job bank a computer database of job listings that can be searched by keywords (p. 15)

Job bidding site a freelancing job site that works like an online auction (p. 153)

Job board a Web site that contains a searchable database of job openings (p. 35)

Job search agents computer programs that periodically search job board listings based on keywords that you provide (p. 100)

K

Keyword a special word related to a specific job and skill that is used to search computer databases (p. 40)

Keyword search a search for a specified word or phrase (p. 49)

L

Listserv a mailing list that receives participants' messages and resends them to subscribers via e-mail (p. 15)

Large organization a company with more than 1,000 employees (p. 27)

M

Metalists Web sites or Web pages that provide massive "lists of lists," or links, to a variety of related subjects; also called meta indexes (pp. 15, 139)

Mid-sized organization a company with 100 to 1,000 employees (p. 28)

N

Networking connecting with people or groups who can assist you in finding a job (p. 10)

Newsgroup a mailing list that receives participants' messages and distributes them to subscribers; unlike listservs, newsgroups have strictly defined subject categories (p. 15)

Niche field a career field that is both rare and highly specialized (p. 2)

Nonprofit career site a Web site that lists job openings for various nonprofit industries (p. 36)

Nonprofit organization a group, agency, or institution whose goals do not include making money (p. 134)

O

Online newspaper an online version of a newspaper; usually includes classified job openings (p. 35)

Open resume banks resume banks or databases that are not protected with passwords (p. 93)

P

Paper resume a resume that is delivered in paper form (p. 40)

Passive job seeker someone who is currently employed and does not want or need employment right away, but is looking for a better opportunity (p. 8)

Personality profile a job seeker profile created from self-assessment questions asked during the job board registration process (p. 99)

Personalized resume a resume that is formatted with word processing software; your traditional formatted paper resume (p. 41)

Portal a Web site that provides links and information to and from other sites (p. 97)

Privacy control over the public's access to your information (p. 93)

Professional association an organization that promotes, and sometimes sets standards for, a profession (p. 135)

Proprietary exclusively company owned (p. 95)

Q

Query a question submitted to a search engine in the form of keywords (p. 73)

R

Regional job boards job boards that provide job listings specific to a city, state, or region (p. 125)

Resume a document that summarizes your education, work experience, and skills (p. 40)

Resume bank a computer database of job seekers' resume listings that can be searched by keywords (p. 15)

Resume "blasting" using a fee-based service to send your resume via fax or e-mail to thousands of companies and/or third-party recruiters (p. 167)

Resume database a computerized storage application for resumes that allows them to be searched by experience, education, job titles, and other elements (p. 10)

Resume seeding submitting your resume to target companies that have no current opportunities (p. 112)

Retain pay a fee in advance for (p. 115)

Retained executive search firms third-party recruiters who are paid in advance to fill executive-level positions (p. 115)

S

Salary how much money an employee earns (p. 29)

Scannable resume a resume that is formatted to be read easily by a computer scanner (p. 41)

Search engine a database of Web pages that is created by computer programs (pp. 15, 73)

Search field a text area where queries are entered, which typically looks like an empty box (p. 74)

Search string a query consisting of more than one keyword that can be modified with searching features (p. 77)

Self-assessment an evaluation, based on several personal elements, that is designed to help you know yourself (p. 17)

Small organization a company with fewer than 100 employees (p. 28)

Spam electronic junk mail; to send unsolicited mail or information to thousands of e-mail users (p. 93)

Specialty site a Web site that posts job listings for a specialized, or "niche," career field or group (p. 134)

Specialty skills skills that relate to a specific profession or industry and cannot be transferred (p. 22)

Spider also called a crawler, the part of a search engine that scans the text in Web pages for pertinent information (p. 73)

Splits systems search firms that share job listings and candidate information and split any placement fees (p. 116)

T

Temping working for an agency that provides on-site temporary workers to various employers (p. 151)

Third-party recruiter an outside party who works with different companies to find candidates for positions that are difficult to fill (p. 10)

Thread a series of messages pertaining to one topic (p. 137)

Traditional freelancing site a freelancing job site that works like a job board (p. 153)

Traditional job search a job search that uses no Internet function whatsoever (p. 2)

Transferable skills general skills that are valuable regardless of the work environment or industry you work in (p. 22)

U

URL (Uniform Resource Locator) the technical term for a Web site or Web page address (p. 15)

V

View when your resume summary appears in a recruiter's search results (p. 163)

W

Web portfolio an electronic collection of work samples, posted to a personal Web site, that can demonstrate skills and talents (p. 42)

Web resume a resume posted to a personal Web site (p. 42)

Wizard a computer guide that helps users through a series of steps to accomplish a task (p. 42)

Work environment the "feel" of a workplace; usually consists of the personalities of its employees, its level of formality, its setting, and its atmosphere (p. 27)